The work-a-day detail
of the
Lewis and Clark Expedition

FIRST EDITION
First printing August 1990

P R E F A C E

This book declared its right to exist. Technically it is a stepchild, an offspring of the LEWIS AND CLARK EXPEDITION (in pageant) which has completed its fourth season. When that pageant was put together, for the sole purpose of glorifying the Journals, people inquired where the book table was. Pageants always have book tables. There wasn't any. There wasn't time to put a book table together. To correct that defiency a slender eighteen-page booklet entitled "The work-a-day detail of the LEWIS AND CLARK EXPEDITION" Vol 1 "The Preparation" was written, printed and waiting. Five of those handy, dandy little booklets covering five different aspects of the Expedition would, in time, be offered to the public. The public didn't want five separate handy, dandy little booklets. It wanted everything under one cover. Therefore the "Work-a-day detail of the LEWIS AND CLARK EXPEDITION" under one cover is herewith completed.

Mabel Johnson
July 1990

For

Captain Meriwether Lewis,
Captain William Clark
and
Sacajewea

CROSSING THE ROCKIES

TABLE OF CONTENTS

FROM THE MOUTH OF the Missouri River and as
far as autumn weather permitted, the mode of transportation for the Lewis and Clark Expedition was pre-
dictable. A fifty-five foot keelboat and two pirogues
would ascend the muddy waters of the Missouri until
winter weather forced the Expedition to lay over until
spring.

In spring when the frozen waters of the Missouri had
thawed, the keelboat would return to St. Louis with
letters to families and friends and reports to the
President of the United states along with scientific
data, specimens of dried plants, pelts of animals,
and general observations of climate and topography.

The Expedition would continue west in its pirogues or dugouts which are boats dug out of tree trunks therefore the name "dugouts". The remainder of the journey across the vast, unknown wilderness of the North American Continent required unwavering faith in the leaders' expertise and their rugged army training.

The path to the Pacific Ocean beyond the Rocky Mountains would be by water, by foot, or by horse-back, if horses could be acquired. Those three modes of transportation would also move several thousand pounds of provisions. Moving thousands of pounds of bulk is a problem under the best of conditions. In the year 1804 it was a monumental challenge. Lewis and Clark's own lives, and the lives of their men, were in direct ratio to those provisions and the judicious dispensing of them.

There were no highways, no trains, no buses, no air-planes, no long-distance means of communication. There were rivers. Where rivers did not flow there would be indian trails, hopefully. There was no plastic to keep men and cargo dry. There was oil-cloth which would stick together, crack and peel and water would find those damaged areas and penentrate. For shelter there were tents made of oiled linen. There were also flat pieces of fabric five feet in width and fourteen feet long to form half-faced tents or to be used as covering for cargo or as sails.

Everything had to serve more than one purpose if possible. Gunpowder was sealed in lead cannisters to keep it dry, lead to be melted to form bullets and dry powder to shoot them. There were other lead cannisters which contained portable soup which the men hated but when their only other alternative was starvation, they ate it. What we know now about lead poisoning maybe it was a good thing that portable soup wasn't popular.

Everything was categorized
such as
MATHEMATICAL INSTRUMENTS
CAMP EQUIPAGE   INDIAN PRESENTS
ARMS   AMUNITION   CLOTHING
MEDICINE

Under the category of MATERIALS FOR MAKING UP THE VARIOUS ARTICLES INTO PORTABLE PACKS was listed "--30 sheep skins taken off the animal as perfectly whole as possible without being split on the belly as usual and dressed only with lime to free them from the wool." Those hides made good-sized waterproof pouches. Scientific instruments had to be protected and provision for that purpose had to be made. The Journals mention that hides of wolves were used for that purpose months later.

The category of INDIAN PRESENTS included 2 dozen

"nonesopretty" (the quotation marks are by this writer). What "nonesopretty" was is a mystery but it was listed after 12 dozen looking glasses, 15 dozen pewter looking glasses and 8 dozen burning glasses. Maybe "nonesopretty" was a common name or the trade name of a looking-glass company.

The most costly item listed in the invoices was "1 CHROMOMETER and KEY" at $250.75 under the category of MATHEMATICAL INSTRUMENTS. There were some ten cent items: "1 saw sett" "1 oz Tartar Emetic" "2 lbs Sal Copperas".

Six papers of ink powder were purchased, 6 brass inkstands. Four metal pens, brass or silver. One set of small slates and pencils. Two creyons (actual spelling). One hundred quills. Lead pencils were not manufactured in the United States until 1861. The ancient Egyptians and Romans had lead pencils with the writing component of actual lead rather than graphite.

The most of any one item bought for use by the CORPS of DISCOVERY were 50 dozen Dr. Rush's pills a popular physic at that time. Purging of the bowels was the first line of attack for any illness in those days. But 600? For indian trade the largest inventory listed was 4600 needles, assorted size, 2800 fish hooks assorted size. The least item of indian trade was two corn mills which the indian men immediately shattered to utilize the fragments of broken metal. The hours of drudgery those corn mills would have saved the squaws was not a factor to consider or even thought of. But President Jefferson thought of it. In a letter dated Washington, April 30, 1803 he states, "I think we spoke together of your carrying some cast iron corn mills to give to the indians or to trade with them-- lest however I should be mistaken, I mention them now."

The final tally of the inventory of indian goods totaled 21 bales. Thirty merchants were involved in assembling the final total which weighed 3500 pounds. A wagon with 5 horses was required to get that cargo on its way. Those figures can be found in Volume 7, pages 231-246 in "The Original Journals of the Lewis and Clark Expedition, 1804-1806", Reuben Gold Thwaites, 1905.

The pages of invoices of purchase for The Lewis and Clark Expedition are factual, recorded history and most fascinating to read. Those invoices were discovered in 1904 a hundred years after the Expedition. Two gentlemen were seeking information on the campsites of the Expedition. They reasoned that the logical place to begin their search was in Philadelphia at the "Purveyor of Public Supplies" where government expeditions were outfitted. To their surprise and disbelief records did exist. Several papers of "Articles wanted by Captain

Lewis" were found and pages of "Articles purchased by Israel Whelen Purveyor of Public Supplies." Those lists when they were layed down for the last time after Mr. Whelen had fulfilled his responsibility slumbered for an entire century.

The payment for those supplies came out of the $2500 approved by congress. President Jefferson did not dare ask for more money than that or he would have been turned down. The final cost of the Expedition $38,722.25.

The destination for all that cargo was down the Ohio River, down the Mississippi to winter over at Camp DuBois on the east bank of the Mississippi across from the mouth of the Missouri River.

The Missouri River was in Spanish domain. The Expedition did not have a passport to traverse Spanish holdings. Britian and France had issued passports for the Expedition's safe passage. It does seem strange that in the wilds of the American frontier that international protocol was such a delicate factor. The Louisiana Purchase was not legal until April 30, 1803. The signing of those papers took place in France. Communication was slow in those days. Two months later the news of the purchase reached the United States.

On December 20, 1803 the Stars and Stripes flew over the Plaza in New Orleans replacing the Spanish flag which had claimed sovereignty for almost 36 years. Captain Lewis was present for that historic event representing President Jefferson. There was a three-week interval when the flag of France flew over New Orleans from November 30, 1803 to December 20, 1803. Again political intrigue.

The territory west of the Mississippi to the Rocky Mountains now legally belonged to the United States. British and French passports protected the Expedition west of the Rocky Mountains. The international legalities now were taken care of but the work-a-day problems for preparation were staggering.

The greatest aggrivation was the building of the fifty-five foot keelboat which was a custom designed job. A boatwright in Pittsburg was hired for that task with the understanding that the completion of the boat had to synchronize with the water level of the Ohio River. Captain Lewis was assured that the boat would be ready by July 20th before the water in the river became too shallow.

Several weeks later Captain Lewis stopped by to see how the construction of the boat had progressed. To his horror and dismay the boat builder had nothing to show. Nothing had been done. The boatwright was a drunkard. When he wasn't drunk he was sick. Captain Lewis reported to President Jefferson, (I have been) "--most shamefully detained by the unpardonable negligence of the boat builder.--I have prevailed upon him to engage more hands. I visit him every day and endeavor by every means in my power to hasten the completion of the work. I spend most of my time with the workmen, alternately persuading and threatening."

Daily the water in the Ohio River grew lower and lower and Lewis was warned by the old-time rivermen that he would never be able to get the boat through on the "lowest-ever" water on the Ohio. Captain Lewis wrote to his President. (The water) "--shall not prevent my proceeding, being determined to get forward though I should not be able to make a greater distance than a mile a day--." How prophetic that statement was!

At 7 a.m. on August 31st the boat was finished, the final twelve days spent on making the oars and poles. "--she was instantly loaded and at 10 a.m. on the same day I left Pittsburg." Eleven men were on board to unload and reload cargo to lighten the load and physically move that fifty-five foot boat over riffles and sandbars. The boat was designed to draw three feet of water. By use of manpower, shovels, rented oxen teams and horses it was at times dragged through

water no deeper than six inches. "--I found it impossible to pass even with empty boat, without getting into
the water and lifting her over by hand," wrote Captain
Lewis.

To save time and spare the fatigue of his men, wagons
and teams were rented to transport the cargo and store
it in areas where the Ohio ran deep enough to navigate.
Sometimes those wagons and teams showed up; sometimes they didn't. The exhausting physical demands on
the men required days of laying over to recuperate. The
Expedition was weeks behind schedule. Captain Clark was
assigned the responsibility of selecting a site for winter-
ing over and constructing cabins.

All the while both he and Captain Lewis were recruit-
ing men, but there were so few who were truly qualified. However, in time, bits and pieces of good fortune
came their way and they assembled a strong nucleus
which became known as "the 9 young men from
Kentucky."

Two of those men were with Captain Lewis on that
arduous descent of the Ohio River. Captain Clark
selected the other seven from different areas. They
were gunsmiths, cooks, handymen, blacksmiths, buckskin
clothing-makers, fishermen, carpenters, indian fighters,
interpreters. They had perseverance and were unfailingly
loyal. They were keenly and quickly perseptive with a

remarkable awareness and respect for the intelligence of their two leaders. Perhaps the finest tribute that can be paid those chosen few who were permited the honor to be part of the expedition is that they were intelligent enough to recognize the outstanding qualities of their two Captains. They were wise enough to know that they, as individuals, were not hired to challenge their leaders. They were hired to support and faithfully follow, an intelligence to which we are all indebted.

There were many reasons for the success of the Lewis and Clark Expedition. The group was a wonderful assemblage of democratic America. German, Irish, French Canadian, French-indian, assorted half-breeds, none formally schooled except George Shannon, 19, the youngest who became an attorney. Their most skilled carpenter, Patrick Gass, was the product of nineteen days of formal education. He kept a journal, all men were encouraged to, and this wonderful Irishman was the first to have his journal published in 1807, and the last to die at the age of ninety-nine years. Mention should be made here of his carpentry. He was an enlisted man and applied to accompany the Expedition but his commander refused to let him go. The army needed good carpenters, too, and no boss wants to give up his most skilled carpenter. Gass went directly to Captain Lewis, who in turn went directly to the commanding officer. Gass was permitted to join the Corps of Discovery. His skill in carpentry kept the men dry and warm through two severe winters in the wilderness.

Then there was Cruzatte, a French-Canadian, who was blind in one eye and nearsighted in the other. He was a waterman of great skill and courage. He knew his own ability and knew how to judge the force and direction and treachery of raging rivers. Even the indians along the Columbia River whom Lewis and Clark deeply admired for their water skills, "the best watermen in the world" could not believe Cruzatte's daring in navigating the treacherous narrows at the Dalles which even they, the Indians, dared not challenge. Perhaps Cruzatte's limited vision minimized the initial danger, but he never failed when he was on the water. His hearing certainly would tell him the magnitude of the water, the roar and dashing of its merciless force.

That same hearing had a delicacy of musical pitch. Cruzatte was one of the finest fiddle players anyone could hope to listen to. Therapy probably was a word not in vogue in the 1800s but Lewis and Clark knew that the men needed some diversion to relieve the brutal physical demands on their bodies. No matter how weary they were at the end of the day, Cruzatte's fiddle playing would set them to dancing. There were two fiddle players at the onset of the

Expedition. A young man by the name of George Gibson brought his fiddle but it was washed overboard enroute.

At Fort Vancouver in Vancouver, Washington is displayed the most wretched looking fiddle human eye can behold. A card states that probably Cruzatte's fiddle was similar to that. It looks like something someone dragged out of the brush.

There is an entry in the "Invoices of Purchase" which is puzzling. Under the category of CLOTHING is listed 30 pairs of socks. When the men signed up for the Expedition they were told that they would be gone 15 to 18 months with everything furnished by the United States government. But thirty pairs of socks to last fifteen men for a year and a half? Actually the Expedition lasted 2 years, 4 months and 12 days. There is another category that lists twenty pairs of shoes. Captain Lewis knew that weight was a concern. He also knew there would be times when everything would be carried on the backs of the men.

The following is a list under the category of CLOTHING for the Lewis and Clark Expedition:

15 blankets, 3 point
15 march coats with hoods and belts
15 woolen overalls
15 rifle frocks of waterproof cloth if possible

30 pairs of socks or half stockings
20 fatigue frocks or hunting shirts
30 shirts of strong linen
30 yards of common flannel

Coats? Overalls? Hunting shirts? Linen shirts? Who sewed those garments? The sewing machine wasn't invented until 1846, almost half a century after the Expedition. Everything prior to that had to be sewn by hand. That included all uniforms in all wars in all centuries. The sewing machine didn't become a mass manufacturing tool until 1865 when power machines were invented.

But some ready-to-wear clothing became an industry as early as the 1830s. The sailors on the whaling ships had to have clothing. In New Bedford, Massachusetts a poor quality of men's clothing became available. They were of the poorest grade possible but they answered a need and an industry was born.

The dealers of men's ready-to-wear would purchase fabric, cut it according to their patterns, then hire women to sew the garments by hand, an effective cottage industry. The clothing was primarily shirts, coats, trousers, jackets and overcoats. They were low-priced garments for low-paid working men. Because of this poor quality "store-made" clothes, for decades, were looked upon as trash. Even during the whaling-boat era those garments were referred to as "slops" clothes.

But Captain Clark referred twice in his Journals to "public stores" after the Expedition returned to

St. Louis from that 8,000 mile round trip across the
the North American Continent. The Captains had
brought with them a Mandan Chief and his wife and
son to visit Thomas Jefferson. Captain Clark wrote,
"--we took the Chief to a public store and furnished
him with some clothing ." And, "--after dinner went
to a store and purchased some clothes, which we
gave to a tailor and directed be made."

Second-hand clothing shops were not unknown. They
existed even in colonial times and long before
colonial times in Europe. Garments could be rented
out, even for a year including hats and were referred
to as subscription clothes. Queen Elizabeth's cast off
clothes could be hired out. A distinguished tailor of
that time complained that the "Yoeman of the queen's
wardrobe" should never have permitted that. Any
person, even of low estate socially, could "hire" a
queen's gown if she had the money. Hiring out
clothes was a regular business with tailors. The
indian chief referred to in the Journals probably was
dressed in second-hand clothing. It couldn't be other
wise. This was a quarter of a century before the
"slops" ready-to-wear were on the market.

The Journals occasionally mention that the men were
busy washing their clothes. They certainly were not
washing buckskin. Then what were they washing?
We have only the invoices to guide us and there is
no mention of underwear.

Underwear is a luxury. Frontier men did not have the standards of cleanliness and comfort which we are permitted today because of underwear.

For centuries women did not wear under drawers. There weren't any. Women's drawers were an evolutionary process born in vanity during the 1840s and 50s, in some places as late as the 1860s. Women did wear an under garment called a chemise, a long, loose-fitting shirt-like piece of clothing next to their bodies.

There is a diary by a woman in Pennsylvania in the mid 1840s noting her reaction on seeing her first pair of under drawers. She wrote, "Why didn't someone think of this before? They will be so warm." Men probably fared better for under garments. Trousers were worn under their tunics in the early 9th century. But even so, for decades any kind of underwear was a luxury. We have only to think back to the 1920s and 30s of our own recent frontier people, the homesteaders. One day prowling around with friends in eastern Oregon we stopped at a small deserted homestead house to look around. The question was asked, "Where are the closets? Where did they keep their clothes?" The elderly gentleman who was a product of those lean years, said, "They wore their clothes. What they owned was on their backs. They only had one set of clothes." Then he added rather wistfully, "Underwear makes the wearing of clothes more comfortable. Overalls are sharp and coarse." Our frontier men, women and children were tough.

The men of the Expedition were also tough and learned a new toughness the winter of 1803 waiting for spring when the Expedition would officially begin. As Captain Lewis wrote in the Journals, Camp DuBois was a time for "whipping into shape.". How those free-roving men who loved their independence and un- structured life style must have rebelled at military drill, lights out, curfew, instant obedience. But obey they did or they were not of the party. There are historians who feel that the success of the Expedition was due to that unyielding hard line of discipline.

Clark was in charge of those rigorous details. Captain Lewis was beset with paperwork, being tutored in zoology, botany, astronomy, medicine, plus the respon- sibility of purchasing supplies, many of which were scarce. "Not a keg can be obtained in St. Louis". wrote Captain Lewis. No red paint could be found to paint the breastworks of the keelboat. (But 200 nails were found.)

Also, there were days when the Captains were unwell. On the trip down the Ohio Captain Lewis complained several times of the ague which incapacitated him for hours with chills and fever and weakness. Captain Clark also mentioned days of illness. Still they pro- ceeded on.

In addition there were 45 men stationed at Camp
Du Bois. They were young and healthy with plenty of
time for inventive thinking which manifested itself
immediately when both Captain Lewis and Captain
Clark were off base to attend to other matters.

Sargeant Ordway was in command when the captains
were absent and Charles Floyd was in charge of the
officers' quarters and stores. Those two young men
did their best but discipline became primarily a word
when the bosses were gone. That resulted in tongue-
lashings and restrictions but the captains were aware
of how bored the men were with this inaction and May
many months away.

For five months those men waited. They didn't have
the leisure time or the pleasant diversions or the comfort of cleanliness we are blessed with today. To begin
with, there were no dwellings on the site of Camp
DuBois waiting for the men to move into. There was
a forest. The trees had to be felled without chainsaws
and those green, heavy logs had to be hewed and lifted
and stacked on top of each other to form log cabins.
The cantonment was pleasantly designed by Captain
Clark with a rectangular cabin at each corner, half
of the cabin extending beyond the log stockade which
enclosed the area. The roofs on the cabins were slanted,
not gabled.

The work in Camp DuBois, also known as Camp Wood
River, was laborious. The men had to be fed. Hunters

were sent out to bring in meat which had to be
butchered and cooked in an open fireplace. The
cleanup which followed three meals a day for 45
men with no running water, no grease-cutting deter-
gent and poor lighting was an endless drudge. There
was no TV, no radio, no recorded music, no books to
read. Communication was by horse, by foot, or by
water. For entertainment there were two fiddles, a
jewsharp, harmonica, a tamborine, and some tin horns.

For five months that enclosure was the Expedition's
world, but the day would come when the gates of
that stockade would open for the last time and the
men would face the unknown wilderness of a great
continent.

For that they would be prepared.

ONE OF THE KENTUCKY NINE

Up the Missouri
to the Mandans

MAY 14, 1804

*"--set out at 4 o'clock p.m.
and proceeded on under
a gentle breeze up the
Missouri--"*

THAT SIMPLE statement gives the impression of a pleasant outing on a placid flow of water. Nothing could have been more untrue. Terrible words had been written about the Missouri River.

"Wild" "Muddy" "Rapid" "Furious"

"Violent" "Brutal" "Toilsome"

"Arduous" "Backbreaking" "Drift-

wood" "Islands of entire trees

entangled together, coming at us"

"Drowned buffalo as many as 30 or

40 a day"   "Unstable shoreline
suddenly giving away, even
from under us."

A French Jesuit viewing the Missouri at the height
of a June freshet in 1673 wrote, "I have seen nothing more frightful." That may have been either
Marquette or Joliet who discovered the mouth of
the Missouri in 1673 on their way down the Mississippi.

The placid Mississippi flowing contentedly at two
miles per hour jolted by 7 miles per hour of the
Missouri coming down hill from the wilds of the
North American Continent a distance of 2,464 miles
of accumulated energy and force. Twenty-four hours
a day the uncontrolable Missouri emptied its silt-
laden burden into the waters of the Mississippi.

A 1911 edition of the Encyclopedia Britannica
claims that the Missouri poured about 500,000 tons
of silt per year into the Mississippi and was responsible for 94,000 cubic feet of water per second.

"--set out at 4 o'clock p.m.--" does seem a bit late
in the day to set out on such an arduous mission but
John Bakeless mentions in his book "The Journals of
Lewis and Clark" that a late-day start was practiced
by the famous Hudson's Bay Company which had

learned over the decades that the first night's camp should be near the point of departure, anything forgotten would not require a long journey back. Perhaps Lewis and Clark knew of that wisdom and respected it. Two horses also accompanied the Expedition, led on shore to transport the carcasses of animals shot for food.

Forty-plus men, a 55 foot keelboat, followed by two lesser boats, pirogues, launched the greatest expedition in American history. The advantage of a "gentle breeze" would be helpful crossing the current of the Mississippi and meeting head on the unruly force of the Missouri.

The keelboat with a square sail and a proud flag of the United States affixed to its stern, cut an historic path powered by the skill of 20 carefully selected oarsmen. The two lesser boats, one 35 feet long was equipped with a square sail and manned by 7 oars. The other, 25 feet long also was equipped with a square sail and manned by 6 oars. Thirty-three oarsmen powering 3 crafts carrying 3500 pounds of cargo established the starting point of the famous Lewis and Clark Trail.

Only Captain Clark was present at the onset of the Expedition. Captain Lewis was delayed with last-minute details in St. Louis, twenty-four miles away.

He would travel overland to join the Corps of Discovery at St. Charles. Therefore, with one captain and three boats the Corps of Discovery proceeded 4 miles up the Missouri to stop at an island for the Expedition's first camp. Whenever possible the campsites were on islands as a protection from indian attack. The oiled tents were brought out and set up and the men's first meal was prepared with the water of the roily Missouri River which filled one third of a wine glass with its mud and ooze which soon brought on boils and dysentery.

The weather remained inclement. In fact, ten days out of the first 17 days of travel, there was intermittent rain. As a rain-sensitive Oregonian there is comfort in knowing that other areas also have rain. Complaints of Oregon weather started early in history. Francis Drake wrote in 1579 "--most vile, thick and stinking fogges--" when he was off the coast of Oregon.

The second day of travel for the Corps of Discovery brought on troublesome problems. The men soon discovered that their boats were too heavily laden in the stern and became hungup on concealed timbers imbedded in the mud of the river. In a ten-mile distance of travel there were three hangups on concealed timber, or sawyers as they often were referred to. To add to the danger, the wild flow of the Missouri's silted water

produced shifting sandbars on which boats became help-
lessly hungup. In "The History of the Lewis and Clark
Expedition" by Elliott Coues, that outstanding works
published in 1893, there is an interesting footnote. "I
traveled in (a pirogue) nearly a thousand miles down
the river from the head of navigation to Bismark, and
found it safe and commodious. It was manned with four
oars and steered with a long pivotal sweep. It carried
a crew of 12 men, besides myself and three companions
with a month's provisions and could be fitted with a
mast and sail (made of a tent-fly) to help along when
the wind was abaft; yet it was not too heavy to be
shoved off a sand-bar when we ran aground, if we all
jumped overboard--an incident that no day passed without." Some diarists record that once the men had jumpe

out they would steady their boats until the swift flow of the Missouri had washed away enough sand to set the boat free.

With all the negative history of that river, especially its silty water, this person was looking forward to some day seeing the infamous muddy Missouri. In August 1988 that opportunity came. The annual convention of the Lewis and Clark Trail Heritage Foundation was held at Bismark, North Dakota. The wonderful opportunity of seeing that silt-laden river was now possible. The temperature was 104 degrees and we were stern-wheeling down the Missouri at the rate of 6 miles per hour. This person was stationed over those faithful paddles to catch her first proof of that historic muddiness. All she could see was beautiful, clear-green water being churned by the paddles. Maybe she had misread the itinerary. Maybe this was a different river. On inquiry of our knowledgable tour guide, this person heard with sadness that there was no silty Missouri water similar to the Lewis and Clark Expedition. The channel of the Missouri had been straightened to eliminate many protruding bends which caused the major problems of silting. Also, today when the water reaches the many dams it is slowed down and in the process the silt load is dropped which greatly reduces the muddiness. The melancholy of that information has not totally left this individual. Surely, somewhere along that great length there has to be silted water representative of the Missouri of historic reputation. Such a reason for melancholy probably never could have been understood by Lewis and Clark, the indians, the explorers, the mountain men and traders wh risked their lives on the great Missouri.

At 2 p.m. on the third day out the Corps of Discovery had traveled 21 miles from its point of departure and arrived at St. Charles to await Captain Lewis. St. Char was a small river town consisting of about 100 small wooden houses with a population of about 450 people. T inhabitants of St. Charles were descendants of French Canadians. Captain Clark noted, "--these people appear pore, polite and harmonious--." They also knew how to have a good time and when 45 young men descended on their village a dance was held in honor of their arrival. Not all the Corps of Discovery could attend. Some were on guard duty which was conveniently circumvented by "absent without leave--." Captain Clark had warned "--each will have a true respect for his own dignity--" which was forgotten by some, if even comprehended in the first place. That was the beginning of lashes on bar backs. Those were not the only whippings for stealing r and getting drunk, falling asleep while on guard duty, spraking disrespectfully, and deserting nor was that type of punishment an invention of Captains Lewis and Clark It was the way of the military.

Weather was a non-ending problem. Rain had dampened the Expedition's cargo on its short twenty-one mile run to St. Charles. The bales had to be opened and the contents dried. The Journals mention many times the need for drying the cargo which makes a person wonder at the condition of the trade goods. By today's standards it must have been dreary. Today we expect all merchandise to be picture perfect, even to the lowly potatoe. But in those days, at those distances, the commodity had priority; the esthetics of the merchandise could be tolerated.

On May 20, 1804 Captain Lewis arrived at St. Charles in a heavy down pour of rain accompanied by some stalwart friends from St. Lewis and a newly purchased Newfoundland dog, Seaman, which had cost Captain Lewis twenty dollars. After changing into dry clothes, Captain Lewis assumed his responsibilities. On inspection of the firearms he found them in need of attention and ordered them promptly put to order. Also, he explained the division of duties on the keelboat:

> The sergeant at the helm, "To steer, arrange the baggage, attend to the compass and see that no cooking utensils or loose lumber of any kind is left on deck."

> One sergeant in the center, "To command the guard, manage the sails, see that the men at their oars do their duty and attend to the issues of spiritous liquors."

> The 3rd sergeant in the bow, "To keep a good lookout for all danger which may approach, either of the enemy or obstructions."

*"These positions are to be rotated
and each sergeant is to have a squad
of 3 men under him. Sergeant Ordway is
to retain his job of issuing staples:*

    Lyed corn and grease one day
    Pork and flour the next
    The following, indian meal
    and pork
    But no pork is to be issued
    when fresh meat is available.

Five days after the Expedition departed St. Charles the men camped near a small French village of seven hous which was called La Charrette, the last white settleme on the Missouri River. The kind inhabitants of La Charrette provided the Corps of Discovery with fresh milk and eggs.

It is interesting to note in the Journals the need for animal fat in the men's diet. Six hundred pounds of fa had been included in their supplies. Eighteen days after leaving La Charrette Captain Lewis had the good fortu to purchase 300 pounds of "grease" at 5 cents per pour from 2 cargo boats on their way to civilization. One b was loaded with furs and peltries, the other with buffa "grease" and tallow. Fat was a vital food in the men's diet. It also was coveted by the indians who were mos reluctant to part with it. The Tillamook indians along Oregon coast in January 1806 did not want to sell Captain Clark any of the whale oil or blubber they ha salvaged from a whale which had washed ashore on the beach. The indians would use the grease as a dip for their camas and wappato-root "bread" which was made from the steamed, small bulb of those two plants then pressed into loaves measuring, roughly 12x12x2 inches. Those loaves would then be dried and stored away for food during the winter. Sizes may have varied from tribe to tribe but that approximate dimension was used by the Clackamas indians on the Clackamas and Willamette rivers in Oregon.

Food continued to be plentiful "--(from) some small willows and bark we made a drag and hauled it up a creek and caught 318 fish of different kind--pike, bass , salmon, perch, red horse, small cat, and a kind of perch called silver fish." On the following day, in the same location, Lewis and twelve men caught 800 fish. One day they caught 3 very large catfish "--a quart of oil came out of the surplus fat of one of those fish--."

Fresh fruit and berries growing wild along the Missouri were plentiful during the summer months. The Journals mention gooseberries; salmonberries; raspberries; service-berries; currants, black, yellow, red, purple; plums; grapes; even cherries which the men picked and added to a barrel of whiskey. Someone must have had a memory of "cherry bounce" a Cajun concoction a sweet smooth, soothing liqueur. There probably are many variations to "cherry bounce" but basically only three ingredients are needed: whiskey, sugar, and fresh ripe pie cherries with only the stems removed. Leave the pits in. Procedure and proportion of ingredients are important and a flat top and bottom glass container. A recipe this person uses calls for two-fifths of whiskey and three pounds of granulated white sugar put into a one-gallon glass container with a flat top and bottom. The sugar must never be stirred. When the whiskey and sugar are in the container the ripe pie cherries are added until the container is full. Then the gallon container is put in a cool, dark place and turned upside down several times a week, not every day. This turning dissolves the sugar which trickles down through the whiskey at its own rate. When all the sugar has been totally disolved the cherries are removed. They now are shriveled and brown, potent and bitter. A senior-citizen friend of this writer loves them but she only eats them when she is making dinner, about a dozen. A mellowing time is necessary, a time for the heavy sugar syrup, which is visible, to blend into the whiskey. This person continues to turn the container which hastens the process.

As early as a month up the Missouri, Clark wrote, "The party is much afflicted with boils, felons, etc." A month later he wrote, "One man with a tumor on his breast." Six days later. "Captain Lewis opened the tumor of a man on the left breast which discharged half a pint."

Other discomforts plagued the Expedition. One of the me

was bitten by a snake. Not knowing if the snake was poisonous, Captain Lewis took no chances, "--to deaden the pain and draw out the venom--applied a poultice of bark and gunpowder--foot swelled much."

Bark and gunpowder does seem rather wild but this person remembers as a child in a remote logging camp in Oregon's Coast Range, of having bacon strips bound to her hand to bring a sensitive swelling to a head. She had fallen on a board and the conclusion was that a sliver was imbedded but there was no way of getting to it. The swelling increassed and the bacon strips were renewed. In time the absess broke and with mild pressure five slivers popped out.

August 19, 1804 a serious illness occured. "Sergeant Floyd is taken very ill all at once with a bilious colic. We attempt to relieve him without success. He gets worse and we are much alarmed at his situation. All attention to him.--Sergeant Floyd much weaker and no better. Sergeant Floyd as bad as he can be, no pulse, and nothing will stay a moment on his stomach or bowels. Sergeant Floyd died with a great deal of composure. We buried him on the top of the bluff a half mile below a small river to which we gave his name. He was buried with the honors of war.

Much lamented. A cedar post with the name

Sergeant Floyd

Died here

20th of August

1804

was fixed at the head of his grave. He was the only man
of the Expedition to die.

The heat became intense. One of the men suffered from
sunstroke. "--Captain Lewis bled him and gave niter whic'
has revived him much." The Journals mention the annoyance of mosquitoes. Fortunately the men were equipped
with mosquito "biers" and could get their sleep at night.
How those "biers" were constructed this person does not
know but in the book "U.S. Army Uniforms and
Equipment, 1889" by the Quartermaster General of the
Army there is a picture and specific dimensions for a
"mosquito bar" made of "quality barred mosquito netting"
in the shape of a box 7 feet long with tapes to tie at
four corners. Whatever the design was in 1804 those
"biers" were made of sturdy fabric as Captain Lewis
states on July 15, 1806, thirty-eight days before the
Corps of Discovery returned to St. Louis "--the mosquito
continue to infest us in such manner that we can scarce
exist; for my own part I am confined by them to my bie
at least 3/4 of my time, my dog howls with the torture
experiences from them, they are almost insupportable, th
are so numerous that we frequently get them in our thro
as we breathe." There also are references to building

smudge fires as a protection, even for the horses
when that mode of travel was used.

George Shannon, the youngest of the party, 19 years
old, had a tendency to get lost. Sixteen days is a
long time to be lost. On the morning of August 26, 1804,
three months and 12 days after the Expedition entered
the Missouri River, Captain Lewis sent Shannon and
Drewyer to look for the horses which had strayed away.
The main party proceeded on with instructions for
Drewyer and Shannon to overtake it when the horses
had been found but to keep to the high country.

Drewyer reported to camp the following morning saying that "--he could neither find Shannon nor horses--
we sent Shields and J. Fields back to hunt for Shannon
and the horses--" and the main party set sail under a
gentle breeze. That afternoon Shields and Fields joined
the party and informed the captains that Shannon had
the horses ahead and they could not overtake him. The
captains knew that Shannon was not a first-rate hunter
and sent a man in "--pursuit of him with some
provisions." On September 11, 16 days after Shannon became lost " (he) --joined us nearly starved to death, he
had been 12 days without anything to eat but grapes and
one rabbit which he killed by shooting a piece of hard
stick in place of a ball. This man supposing the boat
to be ahead pushed on as long as he could, when he
became feeble determined to lay by and wait for a
trading boat--thus a man had like to starve to death

in a land of plenty for the want of bullets or something
to kill his meat." That was not the last time Shannon be
came lost but never for that length of time.

The Corps of Discovery had no problems with indians on
the lower Missouri. In fact the captains were eager to
meet some to inform them that their new "father" now
was the president of the United States and the new
father's flag was different from that of Spain. But no
indians were around. The hunting season was upon them
and they were out on the plains killing and drying meat
for winter. The captains reasoned that there had to be
indians somewhere near and a deliberate effort was mad
to find them.

The Corps of Discovery was now at the Platte River
and the captains knew that the Oto indians resided in
that vicinity. Drewyer and Cruzatte were sent out to
find them. The two men returned in 2 days to report
that they had seen only deserted villages. A week later
Clark wrote "--Drewyer brought in a Missouri indian whi
he met--hunting in the prairie. This indian is one of the
few remaining of that nation and lives with the (Otos.)"
An epidemic of smallpox in 1792 had ravaged the indian
killing them by the hundreds. The few remaining Missou
indians resided with the few remaining Otos who
lived on the Platte River to be near the few remaining
Pawnees for protection. The survivors of the epidemic
were targets of warring tribes. The Sioux were a restle

warring nation, by their own count they were at
peace with 8 tribes and at war with 23.

At sunset on August 2, fourteen Otos and Missouri
indians arrived at the camp of the Expedition. The
indians were given gifts of food, roast meat, pork,
flour and meal. In return, the indians presented the
captains with watermelons. That was the first time
the indians had been invited to the Expedition's camp.
Clark wrote, "--every man on his guard and ready for
anything."

The Council, the following day was successful and
more presents were given according to rank. Indian
tribes were tightly structured. There was a grand
chief, a great chief, first, second and third chiefs with
varying responsibilities. When all had spoken and
promises made, Captain Lewis demonstrated the airgun
to the astonishment of the indians. A similar demon-
stration along the Ohio River when Captain Lewis was
getting the keelboat from Pittsburg to Camp DuBoise,
created a near tragedy. Somthing went amiss and a
woman was shot in the head. She screamed and blood
streamed down her face. On examination Captain Lewis
was relieved to learn that the wound was only super-
ficial.

Ralph K. Andrist in his book "To the Pacific With
Lewis and Clark" states that airguns were rare in the
United States at that time but had been used in England

for 30 years. One historian claims that the airgun was

brought along because it was accurate and could be used
if the Expedition's powder ran out.

On August 23rd, 1804 Joseph Fields killed the first buffalc
The Expedition now was in Sioux country. A council must
be arranged as soon as possible. The prairie grass was set
on fire, a technique Lewis and Clark had learned from the
indians, a custom to alert others to meet for council.
Finally one day three indians were encountered who told
the captains there was a Yankton Sioux village nearby. Th
captains sent Sergeant Pryor and Piere Dorion, the interpreter, with presents of tobacco, corn and a few kettles
to invite the Sioux to council. Five chiefs and about 70
men and boys followed the delegation back to the boats
and set up their camp. "--they brought with them, for
their own use, 2 elk and 6 deer which the young men
killed on the way from their camp 12 miles distant."

That night the indians danced until late. "In their dances
we gave them (threw into them as is usual) some knives,
tobacco, and bells and tapes and bindings with which they
were satisfied."

The following day "--under an oak tree near where we ha
a flag flying on a high flagstaff at 12 o'clock we met."
Lewis gave his prepared speech. He told them that the
the Sioux nation now had a new Great Father. Traders
would be scent to provide them with what they needed.

The Great Father wanted all indian nations to live
in peace with each other and when spring came the
Great Father would like some chiefs to come visit
him. There were many gifts given according to rank:
metals, wampum, clothing and always tobacco. "To the
the Grand Chief we gave a flag and (certificate) with
a hat and Chief coat which was a richly laced uniform
of the U.S. Artillery Corps, with a cocked hat and
red feather. We smoked the pipe of peace and the
Chiefs retired to a (bower) made of bushes by their
young men to divide their presents and smoke, eat,
and council."

The next morning "--after the indians got their breakfast, the Chiefs met and arranged themselves in a row
with elegant pipes of peace all pointing to our seats.
We came forward and took our seats. The Great Chief
rose and spoke to some length approving what we had
said and promising to pursue the advice--one of the
warriors spoke after all (the chiefs were done) and
promised to support the chiefs. They promised to go
and see their Great Father in the spring with
Mr. Dorion and do all things we had advised them to
do, and all concluded by telling the distress of their
nation by not having traders and wishing us to take pity
on them. They wanted powder, ball and a little milk
(rum)." The indians referred to alcoholic beverage as
"milk".

The first encounter with Sioux was successful and the Corps of Discovery now could proceed on. It still had the Teton Sioux to confront.

The work-a-day detail of the Expedition was ever present: "Dried all our wet articles this fine day--some of which was much damaged--we killed deer and buffalo for the skins to cover our pirogues, the meat too pore to eat--the evening is very cold, I gave out a flannel shirt to each man and powder to those who had expended theirs." The Journals mentioned a white oak tree which grew no more than 30 feet tall and the acorns were falling at that time and the men found them very sweet and palatable, not at all bitter which acorns usually are, "--almost every species of wild game is fond of them: buffalo, elk, deer, bear, turkies, ducks, pigeons and even the wolves feed on them."

"--our hunters complain much of the mineral substance in the barren hills over which they passed destroying their moccasins."

"--three Sioux boys came to us, swam the river, and informed that the band of Sioux called the Teton of 80 lodges were camped at the next creek above and 60 lodges more a short distance above. We gave those boys 2 carrots of tobacco to carry to their chiefs with directions to tell them we would speak to them tomorrow." The indians were very fond of the white man's tobacco. They had a native tobacco which they grew but it was not the high quality that the Corps of Discovery enjoyed. Patrick Gass, the carpenter of the Expedition, mentions in his journals, "Their tobacco is different from any I had before seen. It answers for smoking, but not for chewing." Christopher Columbus saw his first tobacco in 1492 when he landed on San Salvador in the Caribbean. Columbus was puzzled by the strange behavior of the natives who had a Y-shaped instrument which they would hold to their nostrils through which they would inhale smoke. He later learned that that instrument was called a "tobacca".

The Teton Sioux who had been given the tobacco, arrived at "--about 11 o'clock (the following day) the 1st and 2nd chiefs came. We gave them some provisions to eat. They gave us great quantities of meat, some of which was spoiled." At first glance that spoiled meat might appear as an insult but 115 pages later in Vol 1 of Thwaites, page 269, in a footnote we learn:

> "--the indians on the Missouri--search eagerly for the carcasses of buffaloes and other drowned animals that float down the river in the spring season. These although rotten and of incredible stench are preferred by the natives to any other kind of food--so fond are the Mandans of putrid meat that they bury animals whole in the winter for the consumption of the spring."

There are other peoples who like meat well aged. In the 1930s this person, living near a German butcher shop saw in a window a complete round of roundsteak which had been in that window long enough to turn purple. On inquiring of the butcher about this meat he smiled proudly and agreed, "Yes, yes, yes." On leaving the shop this person went back to that window to confirm if she had seen correctly. Sure enough there it was displayed like a beautiful picture with nothing else to compete for attention. There were no maggots, no flies. This person didn't patronize that butcher shop because there were things she was incapable of comprehending.

The Tetons lived up to their reputation. The captains invited the Chiefs on board the keelboat to show them things that were new to their world which might be of interest. The Chiefs also were given one fourth glass of whiskey which they were very fond of "--they sucked the bottle after it was out and soon began to be troublesome." The 2nd Chief pretended drunkenness. The captains with five men took the Chiefs back to shore. As soon as the pirogue reached the shore three warriors grabbed the rope of the pirogue and jumped on board and hugged the mast. The second Chief became even more insolent and staggered up against Captain Lewis saying that not enough presents had been given and that the boats could not go any farther up the Missouri--his gestures were of such a personal nature I felt compelled to draw my sword." Captain Lewis signaled to the boat to prepare for action and ordered all men on the pirogue under arms.

> "--the Grand Chief then took hold of
> the rope and ordered the young
> warriors away. Most of the warriors
> appeared to have their bows strung
> and took out their arrows from the
> quiver--all the men on the pirogue,
> except two, were sent back to the
> boat. The pirogue soon returned
> with about 12 of our determined men
> ready for any event. This caused a
> number of the indians to withdraw.
> I offered my hand to the first and
> second Chiefs who refused to receive
> it. I turned and went with my men on
> the pirogue. I had not proceeded more
> than 10 paces before the 1st Chief,
> 2nd and 3rd Chiefs waded in after me.
> I took them in and went on board."

They proceeded about one mile and anchored off a willow island. They placed a guard on shore to protect the cooks and a guard in the boat. The pirogue was fastened to the boat and the island was called Bad Humor Island because they were in a bad humor.

The Chiefs stayed on board that night. In the morning the boats set out early. The bank of the Missouri was lined with indian men, women and children. The Chiefs requested that the boats stop to let their tribe see them. It was a big event in their lives and with proper dignity Lewis and five men went on shore with the Chiefs. The Chiefs were much pleased and requested that the Corps of Discovery stay a second night. To prove to the indians that the Corps o Discovery was on a friendly mission the captains agreed.

An entry of that date reads: "The squaws are cheerful, fine looking women, not handsome. They do all the laborious work, perfect slaves to the men as all squaws of nations much at war or where the women are more numerous   --these people use soldiers who police the village at night and arbitrate in conflicts. One of them whipped two squaws who appeared to have fallen out. When those police approach, all run in terror. At night those soldiers, at different distances walk around camp singing the occurrences of the night."

There were occurrence that were deeply troubling to the Corps of Discovery. The Tetons had had a recent battle with the Mahars. In that battle they destroyed 40 lodges killed 75 men and some boys and children and took 48 prisoners, women and boys which they promised both captains shall be returned. The Journals note "--those are a wretched and dejected looking people. The squaws appear low and coarse but this is an unfavorable time t judge them. We gave our Mahar interpreter some article to give those squaws, in his name, such as awls and needles."

But the trouble makers of the Teton Sioux had not
given up. They followed the boats for four days,
calling out, pleading innocence, promising good behavior but the captains would have no part of them.
Even the Grand Chief had said, of one of the lesser
chiefs, that he a "double-spoken man."

In bitter resignation the Tetons watched 3500 pounds
of cargo disappear up the Missouri. They had cause to
be sullen. They had built a substantial trading businss
with the other indian tribes and the source of
supply was the white traders coming up the Missouri
from St. Louis. The Teton's formula was almost foolproof.
They would stop the traders , warning them of death,
if they dared go farther. The indians then would offer
to buy the merchandise at prices so low it was thievery.
The traders would yield; they were out-numbered. No
way could they survive the ratio of indians against
themselves. The Tetons knew that and had established
a lucrative business based on that fear.

Then along came Lewis and Clark with 45 men, a
55 foot keelboat, 2 pirogues and 3500 pounds of cargo.
That may have been the largest contingent of cargo
and white men that the indians had ever seen on the
upper Missouri. Numbers can command respect. Also,
that keelboat had a swivel gun on its bow, a great
curiosity to the indians and a fear. It is interesting

to note that when the indians were in a position to trade white man's merchandise they had no qualms about percentage of markup imposed upon their own kind.

With all that activity the work-a-day detail still had to be attended to. One of the boatmen had a severe absess on a hip which would not respond to any treatment. The mice had done damage to the supplies, cutting several bags of corn and scattering it spoiling clothing and papers.

Human error was always present. A pirogue had rammed the anchor cable of the keelboat sinking the anchor to the bottom of the Missouri which promptly covered it with mud. It never was found and rocks had to substitute for an anchor. Navigating became an increasing problem because of the shallowness of the water and the many sandbars. "--three quarters of a day to travel one mile--."

The encounter with the Tetons finally came to an end and the Corps of Discovery proceeded on. As they progressed up the river they came to an Arickara Village in the center of a three-mile long island which was covered with fields of corn, tobacco, beans (and) squash. The indians lined the shore to watch the strange brigade approaching. Captain Lewis with two interpreters and two men went to the village. It was a cold, windy, rainy day. The chiefs were given tobacco and were informed that there would be a council the next day.

Many came. "--those indians were much astonished at my

black servant, York (wrote Captain Clark) All
flocked around him and examined him from top to toe.
He carried on the joke and made himself more
terrible than we wished him to do. Those people gave
us bread made of corn and beans boiled (and) a large
bean they stole from the mice of the prairie (who
collect and store them). Those beans are rich and
nourishing--." In a footnote in DeVoto "The Journals
of Lewis and Clark"that bean was commonly called
"hog peanut" or "wild peanut".

In exchange for that food "--we gave them some sugar,
a little salt and a sun glass--those indians are not fond
of spiritous liquor of any kind--they are dirty, kind and
poor, possessing national pride, not beggardly, receiving
what is given with great pleasure. (They) live in warm
houses built in an octagon form (with) a cone on top
which is left open for the smoke to pass. Those houses
are generally 30-40 feet in diameter covered with
earth on poles of willow and grass."

The Journals also state "--a curious custom with the
Sioux, as well as the Arikaras, is to give handsome
squaws to those whom they to show acknowledgment to. The Sioux we got clear of without taking
their squaws. The Arikaras we put off during the time
we were at their towns. Two squaws were sent by a
man to follow us. The Arikaras regard such intercourse
with strangers disgraceful when occurring without the

husband's or brother's consent."

In less than a month the Corps of Discovery was building winter cabins. The site selected was in a grove of cottonwood trees about 3 miles downstream from the first Mandan town. The Journals state: "--this timber is tall and heavy containing an immense quantity of water, brittle and soft." The design of the contonment was a triangle with the cabins sharing dividing walls and facing each other. Fortunately those heavy logs were placed upright. The construction began on November 3, 1804 and two weeks later the men moved in even though the cabins were not finished. Long, cold hours were spent preparing those shelters for winter, working often until one o'clock at night. Lewis wrote, "--we continue to cover our huts with hewed puncheon." Puncheon is split log. The pioneers used it for their famous puncheon floors. According to historian Biddle who worked with Lewis and Clark to write a two-volume edition of the Journals, published in 1814, the individual cabins measured 14 feet square, the walls 7 to 18 feet high. This variation in height was caused by the slant of the roof from high back to front which made possible a loft for sleeping. The loft floor helped hold in the heat.

All told there were 8 cabins, a smoke house and a storage unit. Storage units were much needed. On November 22nd "--dispatched a pirogue and 5 men to the 2nd village of the Mandans for 100 bushels of corn in ears. Did not get more than 30 bushels."

"--corn in ears" brings to mind that corn cobs were sometimes used for toilet tissue before tissue became prevalent. For common folk, tissue was a long time coming. This person remembers Sears Roebuck catalogues in the outhouse. How did the Corps of Discovery manage that bit of hygiene? There is no mention of it in the Journals. In a 1907 Book "Home and Health" we read,"Provide soluble toilet paper as other kinds may cause a stoppage in the pipes. Printed paper should not be used for it is claimed on good authority that printer's ink is often responsible for serious rectal diseases." In that same book, "--a bathroom is not only a luxury and convenience, it is a necessity." There was a woman in the community where we grew up as children who refused to use such a convenience. Her reasoning was, "We cook our cabbage on the back porch."

But to get back to the log cabins. The cracks between the logs were daubed with clay to keep out the cold and drifting snow. Stones were gathered and brought in by pirogue to make fireplaces. By December 1st the cabins were completed and the men set about gathering and preparing pickets for the stockade to close the remaining opening of the triangle. When completed, that fortification, according to one historian could "withstand a cannon ball."

Ordway writes in his Journal, "We dug a vault 100 yards above the huts in order to make or keep the place healthy. That entry is the only mention of a latrine in all the Journals and that latrine was 300 feet away from the stockade. At 45 degrees below zero that could be tough.

But indoors , the men were comfortable. On December 12 with minus 38 degrees, Ordway again wrote, "Our rooms very close and warm so we can keep ourselves warm and comfortable."

With all the building activity the work-a-day detail continued and the first priority was food. Again Ordway writes, "Raised a provision and smoke house, 24'x14' -- (three days later) --our pirogue of hunters arrived with 32 deer, 12 elk and a buffalo. This meat we put up on poles in the roof of our meat and smoke house."

An immensity of meat was eaten. It required, "--4 deer, an elk and a deer, or 1 buffalo to supply us plentifully." Those 45 carcasses provided only a two-week supply. The indians brought gifts of food"--a chief of the first village came down. He packed about 100 pounds of fine meat on his squaw for us. We made some small presents to the squaw and child. Gave a small ax (with) which she was pleased."

Many brought corn to trade. A chief's wife made a kettle of boiled squash, beans, corn and choke cherries with the stones which was "palatable". That dish was considered a treat among those people. One chief who came to visit was wearing 14 rings of brass on his fingers. The Mandans were very fond of brass.

On December 21 the supply of fresh meat was exhausted and a barrel of salted pork had to be opened which was of great concern as that food had to be saved for use when game was scarce. The indians warned of such areas ahead. But Christmas day was observed in festive fashion, "Flour, dried apples, pepper and other articles were distributed to celebrate Christmas in a proper and social manner". Three rations of brandy made dancing all the merrier that day.

At this point something needs be said about the indian trade goods. We have to remember the many tribes and thousands of unknown miles of distance the Expedition had to travel before returning to St. Louis. On their homeward journey from Ft. Clatsop in Oregon the captains' trade goods amounted to no more than could be tied in two handkerchiefs which was of great concern to them.

Also, during the winter with the Mandans there was keen trade competition from other sources. The Hudson's Bay Company of Canada, which shares its border with North Dakota, and the Northwest Trading Company, also of Canada, were very active and generous with the Mandans. For instance, one of the interpreters for Lewis and Clark was given, by a trader of the NW CO. the following articles "--3 brace ("brasse a French measure commonly used in Canada, an equivalent to 5.318 English feet)--of (cloth), a pair of corduroy overalls, 1 vest,1 brace blue cloth, 1 brace red or scarlet with 2 bars, 200 balls of powder, 2 braces tobacco, 3 knives." Lewis and Clark in no way could compete with that degree of generosity.

The trade problem was compounded by the indians concept that all white men were traders which Lewis and Clark were not. They were explorers. Some of the indians may have understood the difference but most did not. Plus, the rivalry between the North West Company and the Hudson's Bay Company was extremely cutthroat resorting to hostile takeover of outlying posts even to murder. In fact, the rivalry became so violent that the companies had to merge to exist.

Trading on the Upper Missouri is a story unto itself. Lewis and Clark had to make it very clear with the Hudson's Bay Co. traders that they could not give a Hudson's flag or metals to any indians on U.S. Territory, which the Upper Missouri now was. The indians had to realize that there was only one Great White Father and that was the President of the United States represented by the flag and medals of the United States.

The Hudson's Bay Co. had a great trade advantage .

It was an old established, respected company which could trace its charter back to 1670 granted by Charles the second of England. Its traders had had years of experience and offered superior merchandise and ruthlessly undersold all others to control the market. The indians soon learned that a "Boston Blanket" was inferior to the Hudson' Bay blanket. But there was one article of trade in which the United States was superior. Guns.

The rifles the Corps of Discovery carried were manufactured at the government arsenal in Harper's Ferrry, Virginia according to the careful specification of Captain Lewis and those guns proved to be so superior to any other gun that the U.S. Army later adopted the design with only a few minor changes. The Journals refer to the indian's trade guns as "indifferent". It is interesting to note that on the indians' fast-riding buffalo hunts, the gun was an impediment even after the indians had shortened the barrel to eliminate part of the clumsiness. When speed and accuracy counted, the indian could trust his bow and arrow, a skill in which he excelled.

Truly, it is a marvel during the muzzle-loading era that anyone could claim victory. A minute and a half to reload a gun was the average time. Pictures handed down to us show the firing of the guns, rarely reloading of them. But both sides of the battle line were limited to the same slow procedure.

According to the Journals, the month of November was

an extremely busy time for hunting along the Missouri. The indians were out in full force gathering food for the lean months of winter. The coming and going along that river calls to mind the holiday activity at our airports to day.

One hunting party of indians "within 2 days caught 100 goats by driving them in a strong pen directed by a bush fence widening from the pen." A large party of indians invited Captain Lewis to join in a buffalo hunt. The "indians hunted on horseback with bow and arrow killing be tween 30-40 buffalo. Captain Lewis' party killed 10, five of which we got to the fort by the assistance of a horse in addition to what the men packed on their backs." The problem in all those hunts was getting the meat back to the fort. Sometimes the men would be hunting 60 miles away. Any meat left unattended over night the wolves would get. To protect the unattended meat the men wou pile logs around it to baricade it from the wolves.

On another day Captain Clark writes, "--killed 8 buffalo and 1 deer. One cow (buffalo) and calf was brought in. Two cows which I killed at 7 miles distance I left 2 me to skin and keep off the wolves. The temperature was degrees below zero--several men returned a little frost bit. My servant (York) feet also frosted and his P--s a little. I felt a little fatigued having run after the buffa all day in snow many places 18 inches deep, generally 6 or 8 (inches). Two men hurt their hips very much in slipping down."

Clark's negro servant, York, did not suffer permanent frost damage. He left a long trail of kinky-haired progeny. The indian men were much impressed with this "black white man" plus his size and offered their wives to him.

The struggle for meat continued but one day with the temperature at 38 degrees below zero, the Journals state, "--the weather is so cold that we do not think it prudent to turn out to hunt in such cold weather." But they did measure the Missouri River, "--from bank to bank on the ice--" and found it was 500 yards.

The activity continued varied. There was so much ice floating in the river, dated November 15th that "--we sent tin to put on the parts of the pirogue exposed to the ice."   "An old indian visited us with 4 buffalo robes and corn to trade for a pistol which we did not let him have."

The mode of travel now (December) was on the frozen river which was not without problems. "--the horses were heavy loaded (with meat) and they not being shod it was impossible for (the) horses to travel on the ice--- men with 2 small slays (were sent) for the meat--2 men were also sent to conduct the horses by way of the plain." "--the horses appeared much fatigued. I directed some (bran) given them moistened with a little water, but to astonishment found that they would not eat it but pre- ferred the bark of the cottonwood (trees) which forms t principal article of food usually given them by their indi masters in the winter season. For this purpose (the india men) cause the tree to be felled by their women and th horses feed on the boughs and bark of their tender branches."

Horse stealing was prevalent even during the cold of winter. The Mandans would keep their horses in their lodges at night to prevent them from being stolen. At night the horses would be given sticks from the cotton- wood tree the size of a man's finger to that of his arm During the day the horses would be put out to graze on grass.

Mandan Earth Lodge

Daily the hunt for meat continued. Captain Clark writes, "--we proceeded on the ice 22 miles and camped. Killed 9 elk, 18 deer, brought to camp all the meat fit to eat and had all the bones taken out. Everyman engaged either in hunting or collecting and packing the meat to camp--I had all the meat collected which was killed yesterday, and which escaped the wolves, ravens and magpies (which are very numerous about this place) and put into a close pen made of logs to secure it from the wolves and birds. The distance from the fort being nearly 60 miles and the packing of meat that distance attended with much difficulty ,we set out on our return and halted at an old indian lodge 40 miles below Fort Mandan--several men being nearly out of moccasins."

In time all that meat arrived at the fort. But there was no rest. On another hunting trip "--the meat amounting to 3,000 pounds was brought up on two slays, one drawn by 16 men had about 2400 pounds on it."

A new medical concern appears in the Journals, "--several men with the venereal caught from the Mandan women." With the sexual practices of the indians, venereal was bound to be widespread. Medical treatment for syphilis had been anticipated and medication was included as part of the medical supplies. A mercury salve was the treatment used at that time.

An experience this person had with mercury should be mentioned. Several years ago some very handsome burlap bags were on sale at a good price at a feed store in Eastern Oregon. This person knew that those bags would enrich certain pageants which were being planned. The sales person volunteered the following information. "I need to tell you that the contents of those bags were treated with mercury." She was thanked for the information and was assured that the bags would be washed. Thinking over that unusual precaution, this person on returning home called a chemical laboratory. "Burn them." "But they will be washed." "Mercury can't be washed out. Don't make any costumes out of them and don't let anyone handle them." Those beautiful bags. That wonderful bargain a total loss. They were burned. Maybe the bags never should have been offered for sale in the first place which makes us wonder about the mercury salve used by the Corps of Discovery. Reference is made to that risk in "Only One Man Died" by E. G. Chuinard, M.D. Mercury had been used for centuries to offset the ravages of syphilis. There was risk with mercury but there were no other choices until antibiotics.

An ugly incident erupted because of the sexual promiscuity which could have defeated the entire Expedition. Captain Lewis writes November 22, 1804: "--I was alarmed about 10 o'clock by the sentinal who informed

that an indian was about to kill his wife in the interpreter's fire about 60 yards below the works. I went
down and spoke to the fellow about the rash act which
he was like to commit and forbid any act of that kind
near the fort. Some misunderstanding took place between
this man and his (wife) about 8 days ago and she came
to this place and continued with the squaws of the interpreter, (he might lawfully have killed her for running
away) . Three days ago she returned to the village. In
the evening of the same day she came to the interpreter's fire apparently much beat and stabbed in 3 places.
We directed that no man of this party have any intercourse with this woman under the penalty of punishment.
He, the husband, observed that one of our sergeants slept
with his wife and if he wanted her he would give her
to him. We directed the sergeant to give the man some
articles, at which time I told the indian that I believed
not one man of the party had touched his wife except
the one he had given the use of her for a night, in
his own bed. No man of the party should touch his
squaw, or the wife of another man, and advised him
to take his squaw home and live happily together in
the future. At this time the Grand Chief of the nation
arrived and lectured him and they both went off
apparently (dissatisfied)--a month later the indian whom
I stopped from committing murder on his wife, through
jealousy of one of our interpreters, came and brought
his two wives and showed great anxiety to make up
with the man with whom his jealousy sprung."

The winter with the Mandans was arduous and deman-
ding. The blacksmiths put in long hours making battle
axes for the indians and mending their broken equipment
"The smiths have not an hour of idle time to spare."
The squaws always brought corn in payment and Captain
Lewis mentions that without that corn he didn't know
how the Corps of Discovery would have made it through
the winter. But all that metal work required coal to kee
the forges burning and that meant the making of charco
Jan. 24,1805: "--occupied in cutting wood to make char-
coal."

The Corps of Discovery had brought with it a sheet-iron
stove referred to in the Journals as a caboose. By the
time the Expedition reached the Mandans that metal
stove was almost burned out and the usable parts were
cut into 4 inch squares. The number of those pieces wee
limited. They were very much in demand by the indians
to form into arrow points or "turn into instruments for
scraping and dressing their buffalo robes."

The competition must have been extremely keen. Each
4 inch piece "obtained from 7 to 8 gallons of corn from
the natives who appeared extremely pleased with the ex
change." That corn was referred to in measures of
gallons which would indicate that it was not "in ears".
There is an entry, Mar.14,1805, "--set all hands to shell
corn." The next day:"--set some men about hulling corn
In another entry corn is referred to as "strings of corn.

by Vern Erickson (from "On A Slant Indian Village," Fort Abraham Lincoln State Park, North Dakota).

Captain Lewis mentions that without the Mandan corn he didn't know how the Corps of Discovery would have made it through the winter.

The dedication to detail in those Journals is a delight. There is even mention of a spoon used to strike an indian's hand for behaving badly.

With all this activity the female world of the indian women had its own rhythm. On Feb.11,1805 a 16-year-old squaw gave birth. The event was carefully recorded.

61

"--about 5 o'clock this evening one of
the wives of Charbonneau was delivered
of a fine boy. It is worthy of remark
that this was the first child which this
woman had born, and as common in such
cases her labor was tedious and the pain
violent. Mr. Jessaume informed me that
he had frequently administered a small
portion of the rattle of the rattle-
snake, which he assured me had never
failed to produce the desired effect,
that of hastening the birth of the child.
Having the rattle of a snake by me I
gave it to him and he administered two
rings of it to the woman broken in small
pieces with the fingers and he added a
small quantity of water. Whether this
medicine was truly the cause or not I
shall not undertake to determine, but
I was informed that she had not taken
it more than 10 minutes before she
brought forth. Perhaps this remedy may
be worthy of future experiment.--"

In two months time that baby boy, Baptiste, snug in
his papoose board on his mother's back would accompany his mother, Sacajawea, to the Pacific Ocean with
the Corps of Discovery. Sacajawea's husband, Charbonneau, was signed on as an interpreter. Her presence
was critical to the Expedition. She was Shoshoni, a
tribe with many horses which the Corps of Discovery
would need to reach the Columbia River.

The winter months continued busy and interesting.

INK RENDERING BY SHIRLEY J. NIEMINEN

SACAJAWEA AND BABY BAPTISTE "POMP"

*"--am much engaged making a descripitive
list of the rivers from information"
(gathered during the winter)*

"Put out our clothes to sun."

"Am engaged in copying a map."

*"A young indian--from a differnt village
stole a daughter from a Mandan village.
--(the father) went to the village and
took away his daughter and (the young
man's horse)"*

*"I pack all the merchandise into 8 packs
equally divided so as to have something
in each canoe and pirogue."*

The day finally came when spring began to announce
its presence, nudging the long sleep of winter.

*March 26, 1805: "The ice began to break
away this evening."*

*"Sent out 16 men to make 4 pirogues.
Those men returned in the evening and
informed that they found trees they
thought would answer."*

*"--men building pirogues; making ropes,
burning coal, hanging up meat and
making battle axes for corn."*

"All engaged about something."

"All hands employed."

*"The ice has stopped running owing
to some obstacle above."*

*"The obstacle broke away above and
the ice came down in great quantities.
The river rose 13 inches the last
24 hours."*

March 6th: "A cloudy morning and smokey all day from the burning of the plains which was set on fire by the indians for an early crop of grass, as an inducement for the buffalo to feed on--"

March 30th: "The plains are on fire in view of the fort on both sides of the river. It is said to be common for the indians to burn the plains near their villages every spring for the benefit of their horses and to induce the buffalo to come near to them."

You Oregonian readers will see a similarity to this field burning, only in reverse.

"All employed preparing to set out."

"All the party in high spirits--generally healthy except vinerial complaints which is very common amongst the natives and the men catch it from them."

"Hail and rain with thunder and lightning. It is worthy of remark that this is the first rain since we have been here since the 15th of Oct. last." (5 and a half months--wait until they get to Oregon)

April 3rd: "We are all day engaged packing up sundry articles to be sent to the President of the United States" (on the 55 foot keelboat)

April 7, 1805: "Having this day at 4 p.m. completed every arrangement necessary for our departure, we dismissed the keelboat and crew with orders to return without loss of time to St. Louis. A small canoe with 2 French hunters accompanied (the keelboat). Those men had ascended the Missouri with us the last year as engages."

A footnote in Thwaites's "Original Journals of the Lewis and Clark Expedition" indicates that Reuben Thwaites had been in correspondence with Eva Emrery Dye in Oregon City, Oregon. "The two men (mentioned above) were Francois Rivet and Phillippe Degie, whom the explorers met on their return journey August 21, 1806. Mrs. Eva Emery Dye writes to us that they (the 2 men) afterwards went to Oregon and settled in Champoeg and was locally celebrated as being men who had been with Lewis and Clark."

Eva Emery Dye was an early, respected Oregon City, Oregon writer. In a 1905 Oregonian she reviews the first three volumes of Thwaites, then adds, "Here the third volume ends, so the remainder of the Oregon's story will have to delay until volume four comes from the press."

After the keelboat had departed, the Journals continue "--we were now about to penentrate a country at least 2,000 miles in width, on which civilized man had never trodden--these little vessels contained every article by which we were to expect to subsist or defend ourselves

Again it was Captain Clark who was responsible for those boats as they set sail, for the second time, up the Missouri. Captain Lewis writes, "I had used no exercise for several weeks, I determined to walk on shore as fa as our encampment of this evening." (later) "--I took an early supper this evening and went to bed. Captain Clark, myself, the two interpreters and the woman and child sleep in a tent of dressed skins. --to erect this tent a parsel of 10 or 12 poles are provided and the leather is then thrown over them forming a conic figure."

This writer in reading the Journals has not once come across any reference by the captains mentioning fatigue or annoyance at loss of sleep because of the crying of a baby at night. It was gentlemanly of them not to complain.

Two days out, Captain Lewis makes an interesting statement. "The pirogue is so unsteady that I can scarcely write." That Expedition has come down as "the writingest" expedition in history. Every available moment would have had to be devoted to it.

Weatherwise the passage up the Missouri had some mild and pleasant days the Journals stating "a fine morning", "a delightful morning". Many times the men would begin their day's travel before breakfast. The flow of the river, at times, was gentle allowing as many as 15 or 20 miles per day. When the wind was favorable the sails could be hoisted and those 8 boats could make 26 miles per day.

But fresh meat was scarce and the quality so poor

it wasn' fit to eat. The area was heavily hunted by the indians.

But the promise of better living was everywhere as the bareness of winter was turning into a gentle spring gree An occasional beaver was shot which had become a favorite food. A good-sized beaver tail could supply "a plentiful meal for two men." The party now consistec of 32 adults and one infant.

Mention is made of an occasional treat of wild onions but if those onions were as small as the wild onions of the stoney Wallowa Mountains in north eastern Oregon, six would be required to fill a teaspoon. But the Missou River onion should have been larger, growing in the rich fertile soil along the river. The amount of fresh produce was limited to what could be gathered nearby when the party stopped for other purposes. The objective was to proceed on, not to picnic. Thousands of miles of travel lay ahead.

The Journals begin to mention the frequent seeing of bears especially the notorious, dreaded grizzly bear. The men had been anxious to encounter some of those bears as the indians related formidable stories of the ferociousness of that animal. The indians dared not hun the grizzly with less than 8 or 10 men to the party which the Corps of Discovery felt was an overstatemen But in time the Expedition also learned to respect the madness of that dangerous animal.

A variety of work-a-day detail continues in the Journals.

A canoe sprung a leak and damaged half a bag of biscuits and about 30 pounds of gun powder. The powder was a serious loss but it was spread out to dry in hopes that it could be salvaged, which most of it was.

Sacajawea knew about the root of the wild artichoke and where the mice hid them. With a sharp stick she probed around collections of drift wood. She soon "produced a good quantity." Those roots varied from one to three inches long and were about the size of a small bullet. They were cooked and found agreeable.

On April 12th we read: "--many flowers are to be seen in the plain".

An interesting note by Captain Lewis: "I walked on shore and Captain Clark continued with the party it being an invariable rule with us not to be both absent from our vessels at the same time."

The beaver now became most plentiful. Those beavers could fall trees 20 inches in diameter.

Violent winds forced the Expedition to lay over. Those winds also blew sand and the men complained of sore eyes. The sand was fine and light and so penentrating that "we are compelled to eat, drink and breathe it very freely."Those weather conditions must have been distressing to a two-and-a-half-months old infant who was exposed to the same elements as the rest of the party.

On May 2, 1805 the Journals record an inch of snow.

A plant called the whiteapple is given a page and
a half in the Journals. This prominence is because
the root, or bulb, was much used by the indians. The
bulb was not easily taken from the ground as it was
firmly lodged in the soil at a depth of four or more
inches. The preferred time to harvest was from the
middle of July to the end of autumn when the bulb
was "--stripped of its rind and strung on small
thongs or cords and exposed to the sun or placed
in the smoke of their fires to dry--those bulbs will
keep for several years, provided they are not permitted to become moist or damp." In their dried form th
bulbs were pounded to a powder and used to thicken
soups. Sometimes they were cooked with meat in their
uncrushed form. They were also eaten raw when green
or boiled then mashed and added to marrow grease of
the buffalo and some berries. Captain Lewis felt
that the whiteapple bulb was tasteless and
insipid, but probably nutritious. The grizzly
and brown bears were also fond of them, digg-
ing them out with their tallons.

Boils are mentioned again and sore eyes.

A surprise encounter with a bear resulted in the
following entry in the Journals: "these bears
being so hard to die rather intimidates us all.
I confess that I do not like the gentlemen and
had rather fight two indians than one bear."

The tow line was much used whenever terrain permitted. "--the safest and most expeditious mode
of traveling, except with sails in a steady and
favorable breeze."

On May 17th the temperature was 60 degrees. The
following morning there was a cold, heavy fog.

Another encounter with a bear, shot through the
heart, but ran "--at its usual pace near a quarte

of a mile before it fell."

An aggrivation of blow flies "--that infest our meat while roasting or boiling, and we are obliged to brush them off our provision as we eat," which prompted the name Blowing Fly Creek.

Repeated mention of the prickly pear begins to surface. "It requires one half of the traveler's attention to avoid them."

Again a wind and sand storm, "--we could neither cook, eat, nor sleep--were finally compelled to move our lodge about 8 o'clock at night to the foot of an adjacent hill-!! where they found some protection. How could a mother care for a three-months old infant under those conditions?

But when there were no sand storms, the air "so pure that mountains and other elevated objects appear much nearer than they really are."

Game was becoming more scarce, particularly the the beaver of which "--we have seen few for several days--". The beaver appeared to keep pace with the timber, as it declined in quantity the beaver also became more scarce.

May 26, 1805: "--from this point I beheld the Rocky Mountains for the first time--these points were covered with snow."

Wood was becoming scarce. "This evening we encamped for the benefit of wood, near two dead-topped trees --a scanty supply and no more to be obtained."

"--our tow ropes of elkskin much worn, frequently wet and exposed to the heat of the weather are weak and rotten. They have given way several times in the course of the day but happily at such places that the vessel had room to wheel free of the rocks and escape injury."

The day came when the captains had to make the mos
crucial decision in the entire 4,000 miles across the con
nent. The Missouri River forked. Which fork was the tru
Missouri, the north or the south? They dared not procee
on until they were sure. "--formed a camp on the point
in the junction of the two rivers--."

From June 3rd to June 13th exploration parties were
sent up those two forks to determine which body of wa
would lead to the Columbia River. Day after day of exploration produced no satisfactory conclusion. From the
stories told by the indians at Fort Mandan there would
be a great falls on the Missouri. The choice had to be
correct. To choose the wrong fork could defeat the entire Expedition. The Rocky Mountains had to be crossed
before the deep snows of winter and already the month
of June was slipping by. To add to the confusion the
waters of the north fork were turbid and murky which
matched the Missouri. Similarity of muddy, turbid water
was a tempting conclusion but the captains had to be
absolutely sure.

The first scouting parties returned. They had scouted
by canoe and by foot. Their observations were not con-
clusive. The two captains, each with a party of men,
decided that they would go up the rivers.

Captain Clark's party returned on the third evening wit
no proof that the south fork was the true Missouri.

INK RENDERING BY SHIRLEY J. NIEMINEN PORTLAND, OREGON

S. J. Nieminen

SCOUTING A ROUTE

Captain Lewis' party arrived fatigued and with no proof that the north fork was the true Missouri. But they had learned that river travel was going to be difficult and decided to store in "caches" as much of their heavy cargo as they could spare and the red pirogue would be hidden and anchored on an island in a thicket of bushes which would release seven men to assist with other duties.

There was much activity in camp, airing merchandise, dressing skins for clothes, getting all guns in order, mending the spring on the air gun, drying meat, evaluating what should be taken and what should be cached away.

When those caches are properly made, merchandise will keep perfectly for several years. The Journals noted: "The traders of the Missouri, particularly those engaged in the trade with the Sioux, are obliged to have frequent recourse to this method in order to avoid being robbed."

The articles the Corps of Discovery deposited were carefully listed:

2 best falling axes	2 kegs of pork
1 auger	1 keg of salt
a set of planes	some chisels
some files	1 cooper's awl
blacksmith's bellows	some tin cups

hammers	2 muskets
tongs	3 brown bear skins
1 keg of flour	beaver skins
2 kegs of parched meal	horns of the big
clothing	horned animal
beaver traps	parts of the men's
	robes

The plan for the next day was for Captain Lewis with four men to go by land up the south fork which the captains had concluded to most likely be the genuine Missouri. Captain Clark was to finish the detail in camp then proceed with the Corps of Discovery to rendezvous with Captain Lewis at some point on the south fork. Everything was put in readiness for Captain Lewis and his men to leave the following morning, even though Captain Lewis was not feeling too well. Sacajawea also was sick; Captain Clark bled her.

At 8 o'clock the following morning Captain Lewis with his party of four "--swung their packs and set forward." By mid day they saw some elk and killed four of them which they butchered and hung up the meat and skins in view of the river for Captain Clark's party."

The sharing of meat along the trail was a courtesy much appreciated whenever the party was separated. The men decided to have their noon meal but Captain Lewis "--was taken with such violent pain in the intestine" that he was unable to eat and had to forego a feast of marrow bones.

By evening the pain had increased and was accompanied by a high fever. They made a camp of willow boughs to shelter from the weather. No medicine had been taken on this short trip but Captain Lewis knew that he had to have some relief from the pain and fever. He had noticed there were choke cherry trees nearby and ordered the men to cut some twigs, removing all the leaves and then cutting the twigs into two inch lengths and "--boiled in water until a strong black decoction of an astringent taste was produced." He drank a pint of it and after about an hour , another pint. "--by 10 o'clock in the evening I was entirely relieved of pain and in fact every symptom of the disorder forsook me; my fever abaited, a gentle perspiration was produced and I had a comfortable and refreshing night's rest."

Captain Lewis' method of medication was not a reckless judgment of chance. He had grown up with herbal cures. His mother, Lucy Meriwether Marks, was famous for her herbal remedies. As a child her son probably had gone with her to the forest, the meadows and wetlands gathering her "simples" which medicinal herbs were called in those days. Captain Lewis knew

what to do when he was dependent only on the gifts of
nature. In spite of his misery he and his men walked
nine miles that day.

The following morning after breakfast and another dose
of herbal tea the men set out at sunrise and by 9 o'clock
had traveled 9 miles. They also had killed two bears
"--at first fire, a circumstance which I believe has
never happened with the party in killing a brown bear."
The men dressed the bears, breakfasted on a part of one
one and hung the remaining meat and skins on a tree out
of reach of the wolves and left a note on a stick near
the river for Captain Clark informing him of their progress.

Before the day was over the men had killed, in addition to the two bears, a buffalo, an antelope and two
mule deer. At sunset they decided to stop. "--feeling
myself somewhat weary being weak, I presume by late
disorder." But not too weak to eat a hearty meal and
"--after penning the transactions of the day amused my_
self catching those white fish mentioned yesterday, caught
upwards of a dozen." Which concluded the day and
ended a 27-mile hike.

The Great Falls of the Missouri were discovered the
following day and Captain Lewis knew that the Corps
was once more on track. Ten days had been spent search-
for that "--sublimely, grand spectacle" 200 feet wide with

an 80 foot drop.

A new schedule now was quickly set in motion. One man was sent with a letter to Captain Clark informing him of the good news. Another to gathering limbs to prepare a scaffold to dry the meat which, hopefully, had not been devoured by the wolves. Men were sent to bring in whatever meat remained. Captain Lewis took his gun to scout the terrain of the river to determine the best place to portage those "sublimely grand" falls and the series of falls above. Everything was set in motion awaiting the arrival of Captain Clark and his party.

But Captain Clark was having serious problems. Sacajawea's condition had continued to grow worse. So much so she was unable to sit up in the pirogue as the party progressed up stream. Captain Clark had her moved to the back of the pirogue where there was shade for her to lie down. The Journals state: "Indian woman complaining all night and excessively bad this morning. Her case is somewhat dangerous."

The party proceeded up the swift current with much difficulty. They reached the camp where Captain Lewis had left "part of 2 bear and their skins." Joseph Fields arrived with the letter from Captain Lewis at 4 o'clock settling the whereabouts of the

Great Falls of the Missouri and requesting "a party of men for the dryed meat" which amounted to 600 pounds.

"--our indian women sick and low spirited. I gave her the bark and apply it externally to her region which revived her much." But that relief was only temporary.

"--the indian woman very bad and will take no medicine whatever until her husband, finding her out of her senses, easily prevailed on her to take medicine--." The day ends: "--we could not get a suffiency of wood for our use."

Captain Lewis arrived at Clark's camp at 2 o'clock the following afternoon and was greatly concerned over Sacajawea's condition not only "--for the poor object herself--with a young child in her arms (four months old)" but also the Corps of Discovery was dependent on Sacajawea to help in getting horses from the Snake indians, Sacajawea's people, to portage the Expedition's cargo overland from the Missouri to the Columbia River. Captain Lewis found Sacajawea's pulse "--scarcely perceptible, very quick, frequently irregular and attended with strong nervous symptons, that of twitching of the fingers and leaders of the arm."

Captain Lewis continued the same medication of Captain Clark. By evening, after two doses of barks and opium and the drinking of water from a mineral

springs nearby "--the pulse had become regular, much
fuller and a gentle perspiration had taken place-- the
nervous symptons abated and she feels herself much
freer of pain--. I believe her disorder originated principally from an obstruction of the menses in conse-
quence of taking cold." The following day we read:
"--the indian woman much better--I have continued
the same course of medicine. She is free from pain,
clear of fever, her pulse regular, and eats as heartily
as I am willing to permit her to of boiled buffalo well
seasoned with pepper and salt, and rich soup of the
same meat. I think--there is every rational hope of
her recovery."

Meanwhile, Captain Clark set out to examine the
country and survey the portage route. The distance
was too great to transport the canoes and baggage
on the men's shoulders. A set of truck wheels was
made, 22 inches in dianmeter, from a cottonwood
tree the only tree within 20 miles which was fit
for that purpose. The mast of the white pirogue was
used to make two axeltrees. The pirogue itself was
carefully hidden and stored in a willow thicket covered with driftwood to keep off the rays of the sun.

Sacajawea continued her recovery: "--she sat up the
greater part of the day and walked out for the first
time--she eats heartily and is free from fever or

pain. I continue the same course of medicine and regimen except that I added one dose of 15 drops of the oil of vitriol today about noon."

Again a cache was dug and all provisions which could be spared were deposited in it. Sacajawea's health improved steadily, so much so she walked out and dug a quantity of the whiteapple (underground tuber) and ate her fill of them, raw, plus a considerable number of dryed fish without the captains knowing it. She had a relapse, the pain returned along with her fever. Captain Lewis scolded Charbonneau, her husband, for permitting this unwise activity for he had strict orders as to what Sacajawea was to do and especially eat. Captain Lewis gave her broken doses of "--diluted nitre until it produced perspiration and at 10 p.m. 30 drops of ladanum which gave her a good night's rest."

The following morning Sacajawea was again free from pain and fever. She even did some fishing. Now all attention was concentrated on the portage which, hopefully, would get them onto the plains where they could bypass the falls and once again continue on the Missouri to its headwaters, thence to the Columbia River and the Pacific Ocean. "--we are about to enter on the most perilous and difficult part of our voyage" wrote the captains.

June 21, 1805: the great portage began. Eighteen miles a day was considered a good days travel on the Missouri. It took two weeks to cover the same distance around the falls.

The prickly pear concentrated its deadly assault.

"the men mend their moccassins with double soles to save their feet from the prickly pear which abounds on the prairie but the thorns penetrate those double soles. I pulled 17 (thorns) by the light of the fire tonight" wrote Captain Lewis. Even Lewis' dog suffered. "He is constantly biting and scratching himself as if in a rack of pain." Lewis continues: "Many limping from the soreness of their feet. Some faint--. The men had to haul with all their strength, weight and art--catching the grass and knobs and stones with their hands to give them more force in drawing on the canoes and loads.--"

"To state the fatigues of this party would take up more of the Journal than other notes which I find scarcely time to write."

Their fatigue was so intense that many would drop to the ground and in that instance were asleep. For 14 days their bodies knew only torture. Some historians claim that luck was a big factor in the success of the Expedition. That the men did not perish from the brutal demands on their bodies does indicate a divine grace.

An unusual incident of survival inspired Montana's famous artist, Charles Russel, to immortalize one of the Expedition's near tragedies. Captain Clar Charbonneau, Sacajawea and baby "Pomp" were caught in a sudden storm. They saw the dark clouds forming and looked for shelter. The only available protection was in a narrow ravine with overhanging rocks where they settled to outwait the storm. Captain Clark writes: "--a torrent of rain and hail fell more violent than ever I saw before. Water was pouring down the hill with immense force tearing everything before it--."

To save their lives they had to get out of that path of raging water. They struggled up that steep embankment. Charbonneau was pulling Sacajawea with one hand while Captain Clark was pushing frantically to get her to safety. Before Captain Clark could pull himself out of the ravine the water was swirling around his waist. In a matter of seconds fifteen feet of water was roaring down that ravine "--with a current tremendous to behold." They would have been swept away and over the great falls where they would have perished. "I directed the party to return to camp at the run as fast as possible to get to our lodge where clothes could be got to cover the child whose clothes were lost and the woman who was just recovering from a severe indisposition and wet and cold. I was fearful of a relapse."

While waiting for the storm to pass, Sacajawea must have been attending to four-months old baby "Pomp" for with the sudden rise of water all his clothes and papoose board were swept away. But baby "Pomp" probably was ready for a larger-sized papoose board and Sacajawea would know how to take care of that.

In that flood Charbonneau lost his gun, shot pouch, powder horn, tomahawk and wiping rod. Captain Clark lost his umbrella and compass. Umbrella--? Whatever in the world was Captain Clark doing with an umbrella on that expedition? Only one reference to an umbrella has been found by this person in the Journals. In that period of time, umbrellas had wooden frames. The covering was oiled or waxed silk or linen and weighed 10 pounds. When whale boning replaced wood the weight was about 2 pounds.

The same storm brutalized the others of the Expedition who were on the plains struggling with the cargo. "The hail and wind being so large and violent--they were much bruised and some nearly killed, one knocked down three times and others without hats or anything on their heads bloody and complained much." The hail measured 7 inches in circumfrence.

July 2, 1805 the portage came to an end "--all well pleased that they had completed the laborious task--." Two days later on July 4th "We had a very comfortable dinner of bacon, beans, suet dumplings and buffalo beef. In short we had no cause to covet the sumptuous feasts of our countrymen on this day."

Ten days later the Corps of Discovery was once more heading west on the Missouri. And the work-a-day detail accompanied them. The niggling, annoying human errors, the inferior quality of work materials, the wildness of the weather, the mosquitoes, knats, boils, blisters, toothache, dislocated shoulders.

Thirteen ax handles were broken in less than one day. The only wood available for replacement was chokecherry which didn't have the strength required to do the job. Things were left behind as the party moved on. Captain Lewis forgot his mosquito bier (netting) and a man was sent back for it. "--it is impossible to sleep a moment without being defended against the attack of those most tormenting of all insects--" A treasured tomohawk had been lost in an extremely brushy area and never found. Another time a man had carelessly left an ax and had to go back for it.

The Journals mention the increased rapid flow of the water and the exhausting efforts to ascend it spending most of the day waist deep in the river dragging and pushing the canoes over the rocks and riffles. At night those exhausted men needed 2 blankets to keep themselves warm even though the heat of the day was oppressive. They longed for an end to the river travel.

Fortunately game was plentiful and the men were well fed. Captain Lewis wrote, "I ate of the small guts of the buffalo cooked over a blazing fire in the indian style without any preparation of washing or other cleaning and found them very good." He mentions the sun-flower and the use of the seed by the indians. After the seeds are parched they are pounded between two smooth stones until reduced to fine meal. Sometimes the indians merely added water to the meal and drank it. Other times sunflower meal was combined with marrow grease and mixed to the consistency of common dough. Captain Lewis thought that combination to be palatable. Also, the sunflower meal was used to thicken soup. An interesting observation in regard to the head of the sunflower should be mentioned. It always faces east. At least it did in North Dakota along the Lewis and Clark Trail in 1988.

The captains now were eager to meet the Shoshoni Indians to acquire horses to transport their baggage over the Rocky Mountains to the Columbia River. The Journals mention that the open plains of the Missouri took on a gloomy aspect. The river was in rock country now, the cliffs rising perpendicular on both sides "--the towering and projecting rocks in many places seem read to tumble on us." For 5 3/4 miles the "--river appears to have forced its way through this immense body of solid rock." The captains named that gloomy, narrow passage "the Gates of the Rocky Mountains." Today it is known as the Gates of the Mountains, one of Montana's prides.

That area was treeless and the Corps of Discovery was

forced to use dry buffalo dung for fuel. An acquaintance of this writer recalls her childhood days in Nebraska sitting reading by the kitchen stove waiting to be told how many buffalo chips to add to the fire to maintain the correct oven temperature for baking cookies. The cooky-baking process moved faster if the mother was freed of handling the chips which eliminated the frequent washing of her hands.

A feast of wild onions is mentioned in the Journals of July 22, 1805. Those onions were about the size of musket balls, some even larger. Captain Lewis gathered about half a bushel of them as he waited for the canoes to arrive. He had chosen to walk on shore that morning. The men were pleased with the flavor of that crisp, white bulb and set about gathering as many as their breakfast stop permitted. The island was given the name Onion Island. A wild garlic was later found but it was "strong, tough and disagreeable."

The water of the Missouri now was brilliantly clear. Captain Lewis shot an otter which promptly sank to the bottom of the river but was clearly visible even at the depth of 8 feet. He writes, "I swam in and obtained it by diving." The party haulted at that place for a noon-time meal. It was then Captain Lewis realized that a thermometer had been left behind and one of the men had to go back to get it.

Sacajawea now began to recognize the country and told the men that this was the river on which her relations live. The men were heartened by the information realizing that they might soon see the headwaters of the Missouri River "--yet unknown to the civilized world."

The serious business of finding Shoshoni indians became paramount. Evidence had been seen: moccasin tracks, recent campsites, willow huts, smoke from the prairie set on fire as a warning of unknown danger. Captain Clark who often served as scout for the Expedition would leave bits of cloth, paper, ribbon and other evidence of civilization along his path to indicate to any indian who might come upon his trail that this was not a war party. Also as evidence of peace, small American flags were mounted on the dugouts which would identify the party as different from what the indians normally saw.

The day did come when the Shoshoni indians were encountered and to everyone's surprise, including Sacajawea, the chief was her brother, Commeawait, whom she had not seen since she was abducted by a band of raiding Minnetarees 5 years ago. Reluctantly only 29 horses were sold to the captains but Old Toby volunteered to guide the Corps of Discovery over a long, difficult indian trail which wound its course in a northerly direction before turning west. This trail was used by the Nez Perce when they crossed the mountains to hunt buffalo and only a few old men of the Shoshoni knew its path. To pursue an immediately westerly course was impossible because of the formidable barrier of the mountains.

On August 1 Whitehouse writes, "At noon Captain Clark killed a sheep--we got it and dined earnestly on it. It being Captain Clark's birthday he ordered some flour gave out to the party." A footnote in "Only One Man Died", Dr. Chuinard states that Captain Clark was on that day 35 years old, the life expectancy at that time.

Captain Clark complains ten days later, "--a raging tumor on my ankle muscle." On that same day Whitehouse writes, "As our fatigues (are) hard we find that poor meat alone is not strong diet, but we are content with what we can get." Two days later, "--as we had killed nothing during the day we now boiled and eat the remainder of our pork--." That was 15 months after those barrels of pork left St. Louis. Luck and divine grace truly did accompany those trusting souls.

The hunger of the men of the Expedition was not relieved when they reached the Shoshoni as the indians themselves were starving and had no food to offer. The Mandans had warned the captains that there way very little in the way of food in the Rocky Mountains, not even bear. The Shoshoni echoed the same warning.

Captain Clark wrote, "If true, is alarming." It was true.

Those Tremendous Mountains and the Columbia

Crossing the Wilkerhoot Mountains Jan 1855

AGAIN A FURTIVE cache was dug to lighten the load and the dugouts had rocks placed in them and sunk to the bottom of the river to keep them from drying out. Captain Lewis took care of those details while Clark and 11 men scouted the proposed route to satisfy themselves that the path ahead was as grim as the Shoshoni indicated. What they discovered was truly alarming, even to those stalwarts of rugged travel.

Through rain, snow and sleet Old Toby led this party of trusting men through the rugged Bitterroot Mountain along hillsides so steep and paths so narrow that horses lost their footing and fell from the trails. "This day we passed over immense hills and some of the worst roads that ever horses passed. Our horses frequently fell." And all the while, along every tortuous mile a sixteen-year-old mother with an infant in her arms traveled with them.

One day the mountains opened onto a wide valley where the party met some Flathead indians whose heads were not flat. Those indians were friendly and shared their food of berries and roots and sold the captains fresh horses. There was no lingering, only the necessary time to make those purchases and the party continued its northerly trek for 7 unbearable days.

Captain Clark writes, "--I have been wet and as cold in every part as I ever was in my life. Indeed I was at one time fearful my feet would freeze in the thin moccasins which I wore. We camped in a thickly timbered bottom which was scarcely large enough for us to lie level. Men all wet, cold and hungry." That would have included Sacajawea whose body needed food to provide nurishment for her nursing baby.

Bleak entries appear in the Journals:

"Killed nothing in these mountains of stone."

"The party reduced and much weakened for the want of food."

"Passed on the side of rocks where one false step of a horse would be certain destruction."

"One of the pack horses with his load was missing. The load of the horse was of considerable value consisting of merchandise and all my stock of winter clothing. Men were sent back over that treacherous trail to find the horse but they were unsuccessful."

"There was little grass for our horses." and water was at a distance.

"Great quantities of timber had fallen and so obstructed our road that it was almost impossibl to pass."

"Killed a few pheasants which together with the balance of our horse meat and some crawfish which we obtained in the creek enable us to make one more hearty meal, not knowing where the next was to be found."

"Sent out all the hunters in different directions. The hunters all returned without anything."

"I am very sick today and puke which relieves me."

Illness was rampant with the men. At one time 3/4 of the men were sick.

Their guide and the indian who accompanied him must have brought dogs with them. Patrick Gass wrote, "the indian dogs are so hungry and ravenous that they eat 4 or 5 pairs of moccasins last night." Whitehouse notes, "men without sox wrapped rags on their feet" "we laid down and slept, wet hungry and cold" "we dined and suped on a scant proportion of portable soup

(sealed in lead cannisters which Lewis had
bought in Philadelphia. The men hated it.)--
also a little bears oil and about 20 pounds
of candles from our stock of provisions."
Those candles would not have been petroleum-based
candles we know today. They probably were made
of tallow.

But the day came when the Corps of Discovery left the tortuous high ridges of the Bitterroot Mountains "the most terrible mountains I have ever beheld" for a gentler terrain. They startled some Nez Perce indians, near present-day Orofino, Idaho, who noted their weakened condition and gave the men pounded dry salmon and camas root which made them violently ill. "Captain Lewis and myself eat a supper of roots boiled which filled us so full of wind that we scarcely able to breathe all night."

In time, in spite of their diet of pounded fish and camas, the men's strength slowly returned. The captains began buying dogs from the indians for food which prompted Gass to write, "we find (the dogs) strong wholesome diet." "game is very scarce and our hunters unable to kill meat."

The men who were able to work started making dugout canoes, 5 of them to take the Corps on its way to the Columbia, thence to the Pacific Ocean.

The captains made satisfactory arrangements with the
Nez Perce indians to leave the Corps' horses with the
indians to be picked up on the homeward journey.
"--collected all our horses and branded them and
delivered them to the men who were to take charge
of them. They promised to be attentive to our horses
until we should return." The brand read,"U.S. Capt. M.
Lewis." The brand was found in 1892 on an island three
and a half miles above The Dalles of the Columbia.

Once more everything was in readiness to proceed on.
"Had all our saddles collected, a hole dug and in the
night buried them, also a canister of powder and a bag
of balls."   "All the canoes in the water. (The Clearwa
River) We load and set out."   "We purchased fish and
dogs. All the men relish the flesh of the dog." Not
Captain Clark.

Old Toby, the faithful Shoshoni guide and his son who
brought the Corps safely across the treacherous Bitterroot Mountains accompanied the men down the Clearwater River. Toby kept himself busy when not traveling. Clark wrote, "Our Shoshoni guide employed himse
making flint points for his arrows."

Then one day the captains were informed that Old
Toby and his son "--had been seen running up the rive
we could not account for the cause of his leaving us a
this time, without receiving his pay for the services he
had rendered us or letting us know anything about his
intentions. We requested a chief to send a horseman

after our old guide, to come back and receive his pay which (the old chief) advised us not to do as his nation would take his things from him before he passed their camp."

The Corps of Discovery bid farewell to the Clearwater when it entered the Snake River on October tenth near present-day Lewiston, Idaho. The waters of the Snake, Whitehouse wrote, were "--swifter than any horse could run."

October 14,1805. "--our stern canoe, in passing through a short rapid--ran on a smooth rock and turned broadside. The men got out on the rock--the canoe filled and sank. A number of articles floated out such as the men's bedding, clothes and skins, the lodge (the captains' tent) the greater part of which were caught by two of the canoes--. In about an hour we got the men to shore with the loss of some bedding, tomahawk, shot pouches, skins, clothes, all wet. We had every article exposed to the sun to dry on the island.

"In this island (where they made camp) we found some split timber, the part of a house which the indians had very securely covered with stones. We also observed a place where the indians had buried their fish. We have made it a point at all times not to take anything belonging to the indians, even their wood. But at this time we are compelled to violate that rule and take a part of the split timber--for firewood as no other is to be found in any direction. "

Six days later they reached the Columbia. "After gettin safely over the rapids and having taken dinner, set out and proceeded 7 miles to the junction of the river (Snake) and the Columbia."

Some historians feel that there should have been expressions of jubliation at having reached the Great River of the West, the final river of the Corps' arduous journey. It does seem strange in view of the fact that Lewis was surprised that Sacajawea showed no emotion when the Corps of Discovery reached the area in which Sacajawea lived as a child before her abduction.

Be that as it may, the Corps lingered at this junction campsite taking advantage of a day of rest "--to mend their clothes, dress skins and put their arms in complete order--an object always of primary concern, but particularly at this moment when we are surrounded by so many strangers" two hundred in one group.

While the men were busy in camp, the captains were recording the vocabulary of this new tribe of indians describing dress, houses, disposition and attitudes.

Those indians were the true Flatheads, their heads had been compressed in infancy to form a broad, straight line from the nose to the top of the head which at the apex measured approximately 2 inches from front to back. These indians were kindly people. "Two chiefs brought sticks of willow and some small bushes for fuel." A truly generous gesture. One man gave about 20 pounds of very fat, dried horsemeat.

The women's dress, or lack of, was a startling contrast with the traditional leather dress of the indians across the continent. "--females have no other covering but a truss or piece of leather tied around them at their hips and drawn tight between their legs and fastened before so as barely to hide those parts which are so sacredly hid and secured by our women."

The houses "--are made of large mats of rushes and are generally of square or oblong form." a convenient material which made dismantling easy. Some of those mat-houses had flat roofs, some were handsomely gabled, while others, temporary shelters, were mere wrap-arounds.

Surprisingly, the men of that nation, helped with the cooking "--first he brought in a piece of a drift log of pine and with a wedge of the elk horn and a mallet of stone, curiously carved, he split the log into small pieces and layed it open on the fire on which he put round stones. A woman handed him a basket of water and a large salmon about half dried. When the stones were hot he put them into the basket of water with the fish which was soon sufficiently boiled for use. It was then taken out, put on a platter of rushes neatly made and set before me." Each man of the party was thus honored. The men found the salmon to be delicious.

Mention is made of one group of indians drying salmon "--and prickly pear (cactus) to burn in winter." By sign

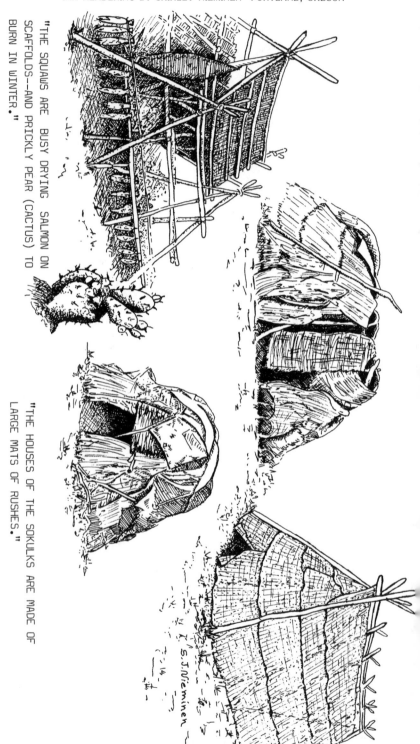

"THE SQUAWS ARE BUSY DRYING SALMON ON SCAFFOLDS—AND PRICKLY PEAR (CACTUS) TO BURN IN WINTER."

"THE HOUSES OF THE SOKULKS ARE MADE OF LARGE MATS OF RUSHES."

language the captains learned that in addition to drying salmon for food they also used the dried fish for fuel. "I do not think it at all improbable that those people make use of dried fish as fuel."

The fall run of salmon was at its height and the vivid pink of those beautiful fish was visible in every indian camp where the squaws were busy drying the fish on scaffolds.

"This river is remarkably clear and crowded with salmon in many places--I observed great numbers of salmon dead on the shore, floating on the water and in the bottom which can be seen at the depth of 20 feet. The cause of the immense number of dead salmon I can't account for--I must have seen 300 or 400 dead and many living." This was normal, for salmon die after spawning but the Corps of Discovery didn't know that.

The following morning, Oct. 18, 1805 "--we resumed our journey in the presence of many--who came to witness our departure. The morning was cool and fair and the wind from the southeast."

They were now on the Columbia, the river which flowed directly into the Pacific Ocean, for which all those months of preparation and relentless struggle were intended. The goal now was in sight.

> Where rolls the Oregon
> And hears no sound
> Save its own dashings

At one time the Columbia River was called the
Ouroagan, presumably after a tribe of indians. It was
a river which inspired many. William Cullen Bryant, one
of America's distinguished poets, included those beautiful lines in his famous poem "Thanatopsis". The Corps
of Discovery may not have known the poetic river-
word "dashings" but it certainly experienced them.

Before leaving their campsite at the junction of the
Snake and Columbia Rivers "--we procured from the
principal chief--a sketch of the Columbia and the tribes
of his nation living along its banks." It is truly question-
able if the Expedition could have crossed the continent
without the help of the indians. True, there were trouble
some ones. There are troublesome people in all nations,
of all colors, in all parts of the world.

Proceeding down the Columbia the Corps encamped along
the Washington shore of the river which gives that state
claim to 450 miles of that historic trail. Montana claims
2,000 miles. Oregon claims the winter quarters at Fort
Clatsop.

A change in indian apparel was noticed as the Corps
proceeded down the Columbia, "--a short robe falling
from the neck so as to cover the front of the body as
low as the waist.
"--their robes do not reach lower than the waist; indeed
3/4 of them have scarcely any robes at all. The dress
of the females is equally scanty for they wear only a
small piece of robe which covers their shoulders and

neck and reaches down the back to the waist where it is attatched by a piece of leather tied tight around the body. Their breasts--are thus exposed to view--."

Also evidence of white-man trade was noticed. "--here we saw 2 scarlet and a blue cloth blankets, also a sailor jacket."

On the 3rd day down the Columbia Captain Clark wrote, "--could not cook breakfast before we embarked for want of wood or something to burn." The party stopped at an

indian village of 8 lodges and bought, at a high rate, some wood to cook their breakfast of boiled dog and fish.

There is a refreshing note in the Journals, "One of our party, Collins, presented us with some very good beer made of the camas bread which had been frequently wet, molded and soured."

Such pleasantness was short lived. The Expedition now was approaching "the long narrows" which brought the men to Celilo Falls which required five days to portage. And here they encountered fleas "--which were so thick among the straw and fish skins at the upper part of the portage--that every man of the party was obliged to strip naked during the time of taking over the canoes, that they might have an opportunity of brushing the fleas off their legs and bodies." Our present civilization has so many protections and comforts.

Busy as the captains were they still took time to note lesser detail. Pole cats (skunks) were in abundance.

CELILO FALLS 1903

The skunks lived in the cliffs along the river and fed on the offal of the indian fishing areas.

The "short narrows", The Dalles, were less than 5 miles away where the waters of the Columbia raged in protest at being walled by massive rock formations which did not yield an inch. To portage heavy dugouts on those treacherous rocks was impossible. A consultation was held with Cruzatte who was blind in one eye and near-sighted in the other, but still the Corps' most experienced, skilled waterman. Cruzatte concluded that with good handling the canoes could be taken through the racing, slashing water. The dangers were noted. "--a tremendous black rock presented itself high and steep appearing to choke up the river. At this place the water of this great river is compressed into a channel between 2 rocks not exceeding 45 yards wide and continues for 1/4 mile when it again widens--accordingly I determined to pass through the place not withstanding the horrid appearance of the agitated gut, swelling, boiling and whorling in every direction, which from the top of the rock did not appear as bad as when I was in it. However we passed safe to the astonishment of all the indians who were, according to the captains "the most skilled watermen in the world."

John Muir, (1838-1914) instrumental in founding our national park system, probably wrote the best description of the transformation of the Columbia River after it passed The Dalles.

> "A few miles below the Dalles the
> storm-tossed river gets itself to-
> gether again, looks like water, be-
> comes silent and with stately tran-
> quil deliberation goes on its way,
> out of the region of sage and sand
> into the Oregon woods."

"Into the Oregon woods" included the infamous rapids
of the Cascades more commonly known as the "long
rapids" "long shute" "great shute". Captain Clark wrote

"--we got the 4 large canoes over by slipping them
over rocks on poles placed across from one rock to
another." That trecherous strip of river-travel now
slumbers peacefully under the placid waters of
Bonneville Dam. After 1896, the opening of Cascade
Locks, portaging was no longer necessary.

As the Corps of Discovery cleared the "great shute"
on the Columbia, the captains became aware of
tidewater. Also was noted a very high, large rock
800 feet above water level, detached from the
Washington shore. The Journals refer to that rock
as Beaten Rock. Today it is called Beacon Rock, the
second largest monolith in the world, second to the
Rock of Gibraltar. A word of caution to hikers, if
you climb that rock, stay on the paths. There's poison
oak up there. In the summer time there are also
delicious, red, ripe thimbleberries to quench your
thirst.

Thirst became a problem with the Corps of Discovery. Water always was dipped from the rivers for use but river water mixed with salty ocean water acted as a purgative and many became sick. Kettles were set out to catch rain water.

On Wappato Island (Sauvies Island) the Corps found an abundance of wappato root, an under water root very similar to the potato, light tan in color but only one and one-half to two inches long. The indian women wade out into the ponds with a canoe and stand in water breast high to loosen the bulbs with their toes. The bulbs rise to the surface and are thrown into the canoe. Hour after hour the indian women tend to this harvesting.

"The indians roast (the roots) in the embers until they become soft--(they have) an agreeable taste and answer very well in place of bread. We purchased about four bushels."

Also on this Wapato Island "We landed at a village of 25 houses. Twenty-four of those houses were thatched with straw and covered with bark. The other house is built of boards", wooden boards made by indians along the Columbia River. Tools of bone and stone, native intelligence and old-growth trees with straight, true grain produced this surprise product of civilization. The length of the board or plank was determined by cutting deep and wide into a tree to make room to insert wedges to begin the vertical splitting process. Some boards actually were split from trees while the tree was still a live, standing tree. Ingenious methods finished the splitting process.

Those board houses were gabled, had ridge poles, supports and plank-covered roofs held in place with cedar withes. (Do get the book CEDAR by Hilary Stewart. The locale is primarily the far northwest coast from Washington to Alaska but some of the techniques probably were similar.

Lewis and Clark saw their first indian-made wooden houses on October 24, 1805, seven days after they

started down the Columbia after leaving the Snake River. "--the first wooden houses in which indians have lived since we left those in the vicinity of the Illinois." Some of the wooden houses Lewis and Clark saw were sort of cellars six feet underground their walls lined with boards.

"I counted 52 canoes on the bank in front of this village."

The indian men "--had scarlet and blue blankets, sailor jackets, overalls, shirts and hats independent of their usual dress--(also) muskets or pistols and tin flasks to hold their powder--those fellows we found assuming and disagreeable, however we smoked with them and treated them with every attention and friendship."

"We proceeded on until one hour after dark with a view to get clear of the natives who (were) constantly about us and troublesome."

"They all have flattened heads, both men and women. (They) live principally on fish and wapato roots. They are thievishly inclined--."

"I slept very little last night for the noise during the whole of the night by the swans, geese, white and grey brant, ducks etc.--they were immensely numerous and their noise horrid." But never a complaint of a crying infant.

The waters of the Columbia now became alarmingly dangerous. The winds, the tides, the rain, the raging storms, the absence of beaches large enough to accomodate 31 men, 5 canoes, a mother and infant. The Journals record a merciless trail of misery.

"No place for several miles sufficiently large and level for our camp--we at length landed at a place which by moving the stones we made a place sufficiently large for the party to lie level on the smaller stones clear of the tide--we are all wet and disagreeable, had large fires made on the stone and dried our bedding and kill fleas which collected in our blankets at every old village we encamped near."

The captains were fearful that the canoes would be crushed by the drift trees which the tide and winds loosened and tossed about. Some of those trees were 200 feet long and from 4 to 7 feet in diameter.

"Our camp entirely under water during the height of the tide. Every man as wet as water could make them."
"At this dismal point we must spend another night as the wind and waves are too high to proceed."

"We are truly unfortunate to be compelled to be four days nearly in the same place at a time that our days are precious to us."

"Our situation is truly a disagreeable one, our canoes in one place at the mercy of the waves our baggage in another and ourselves and party scattered on drift trees of immense size and are on what dry land they (the par can find in the crevices of the rocks and hill sides."

"It would be distressing to a feeling person to see our situation at this time all wet and cold with our bedding also wet."

"--rained all the last night, we covered ourselves as well as we could with elk skins and set up the greater part of the night all wet. I lay in the wet, very cold."

"--winds violent. Trees falling in every direction. Whirl winds with gusts of rain, hail and thunder. This kind of weather lasted all day. Certainly one of the worst days that ever was."

"Our party has been wet for 8 days and is truly disagreeable, their robes and leather clothes are rotten from being continually wet. Our situation is dangerous-- can neither get out to hunt, return to a better situation or proceed on."

"--if we have cold weather before we can kill and dres skins for clothing the bulk of the party will suffer very much."

NOV 7, 1805.   "Cloudy, foggy morning. Fog so thick we could not see across the river."

"--we set out piloted by an indian dressed in a sailor's dress, to the main channel of the river. The tide being in we should have found much difficulty in passing into the main channel from behind those islands without a pilot."

The Expedition would have failed long before reaching the Columbia without the help of caring indians.

Then on that same murky November 7th the fog lifted.

"Ocean in view! O! the joy!"

"Great joy in camp. We are in view of the ocean, this great Pacific Ocean which we been so long anxious to see and the roaring or noise made by the waves breaking on the rocky shores may be heard distinctly."

As the party tried to proceed down river, sometimes only half a mile before being forced ashore by the fury of the waves, the captains accepted that to proceed by boat was prohibitive and on seeing a sizeable beach, landed.

To their great comfort they discovered boards from an old Chinookan village and erected protective shelters. "--our men all comfortable in the camps they have made of the boards they found."

Their good fortune extended into the following day. The morning was clear and beautiful. "We therefore put out all our baggage to dry and sent several of the party to hunt who brought in 2 deer, 1 crane, some geese and ducks, several brants." Wappato roots were purchased from 4 indians who stopped by their camp, a welcome "addition to our food" which had been molded, pounded fish which the captains had bought at The Dalles.

The included map gives a good picture of the progress and dates of the exploration to "the main Ocean" and Cape Disappointment so named by John Mears, the British sea captain who in 1788 thought he had failed to find the River of the West, not realizing that the bay sheltered the mouth of the mighty Columbia.

The sheltering qualities of that bay did not totally

apply to the Corps of Discovery. But the party did linger on the beach where the shanty town of board structures gave them the only weather-protection they had experienced since reaching tidewater on Oct 31 in the vicinity of Beacon Rock on their way down the Columbia.

Most of the exploring from Point Ellice along the shore of present-day Baker's Bay and north to Long Beach, Washington was done by foot.

While camped at Point Ellice, Sacajawea played an important roll in a game of barter. The captains had covetous eyes on a fur robe made of 2 sea otter skins--"the finest fur I ever saw" wrote Patrick Gass. Blankets, red and white beads, a handkerchief, a silver dollar, even Captain Clark's watch were offered. No. Beads. Blue beads. Chief beads. Clark wrote, "The object of foreign trade--are the blue beads--and of those beads we have but few."

However, Sacajawea was wearing her belt of blue beads. She untied it, gave it to Captain Lewis who gave it to the bartering indians and the sea otter robe changed hands. Sacajawea was given a "coat of blue cloth" in exchange for her generosity.

The serious business of establishing a camp for winter became paramount. Indians had told the captains that the south shore of the Columbia had a milder climate and many more elk and deer,

A meeting was called and all were permitted to vote. Sacajawea wanted to be near "pota" (wappato). Captain

Clark wanted to go back to The Dalles. He disliked the seacoast. "---salt water I view as an evil in as much as it is not healthy." Two men wanted to return to Quicksand River (Sandy River) at present-day Troutdale. The east winds howling down that gorge during the winter months would have brought daily regret. Old-timers note the wind only when the water in the toilet bowl takes on wave action, or when windows are blown out.

The remarkable thing about the voting process was back in 1805 a woman was given permission to vote in an all-male assembly. The first woman to vote in Oregon, an indian squaw. Captain Clark's negro servant, York, also was permitted to vote. There were many reasons for the greatness of Lewis and Clark.

Other certain factors had to be considered, too. Availability of elk or deer which would provide meat, the main food of their diet. Nearness to a possible trade ship for the purpose of purchasing trade supplies for the journey home. A warm climate as clothing was scarce, remember the pack horse which was lost on Lolo Pass carried most of their winter clothing. Nearness to a supply of salt to enhance their food and for food preservation.

The captains decided to investigate and the Corps of Discovery crossed over to the south side of the Columbia River.

On November 29th Lewis and 5 of the men set out

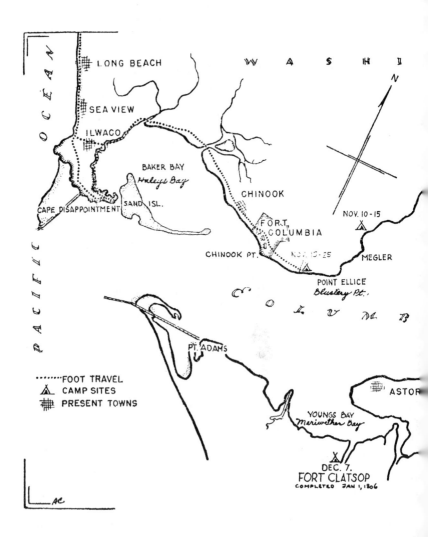

This sketch map shows the mouth of the Columbia River somewhat as it is tod The Lewis and Clark campsites of November 7, 8-9, 10-15, 15-25, 25, 26, 27, a December 7 are indicated. Some names which the explorers gave to promine shoreline points are included with the modern names. Acknowledgment is mo of the valuable assistance which Dr. J. Neilson Barry of Portland, Oregon, gave the preparation of this map.

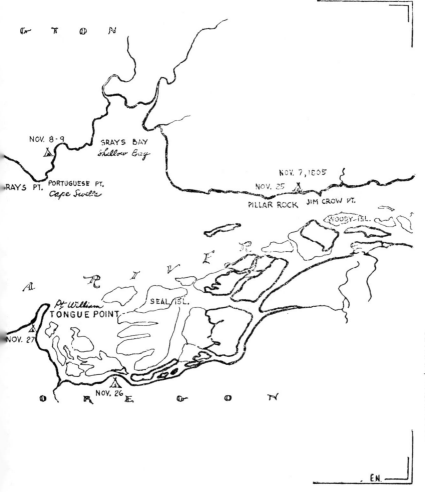

WASHINGTON STATE PARKS AND RECREATION COMMISSION
OLYMPIA, WASHINGTON

correction
as suggested by WASHINGTON STATE
PARKS AND RECREATION COMMISSION
November 15-24 (not November 15-25)
November 10-14 (not November 10-15)

in search of an "eligable place for our winter quarters." December 2nd an elk was shot, the first elk killed by the Corps west of the Rocky Mountains. Five days later seven hunters agreed that elk "is in great abundance on the Oregon side."

In time Captain Lewis found a desirable location on a rise about 30 feet higher than the high tide level and thickly covered with lofty pines (firs) about 200 feet from a fresh water river. On that site less than five miles from present Astoria is the reconstructed Fort Clatsop built in 1955 by three qualified Finnish log-cabin builders.

CAMAS   WAPPATO   ONION

FORT CLATSOP

(winter of 1805-1806)

Fort Clatsop
and the
Journey Home

CAPTAIN LEWIS: "My principal object is to look out a place to make salt, blaze the road that the men out hunting might find the direction to the Fort if they should get lost in cloudy weather, and see the probability of game in that direction for the support of the men we shall send to make salt."

Work immediately began on their cabins for the winter.

"We continue building our houses of the straightest

and most beautifullest logs--which makes the finest puncheon I have ever seen. They can be split 10 feet long and 2 feet broad, no more than an inch and a half thick."

"All employed in finishing a house to put meat into-- we hang the meat up over a small smoke."

"The men are thinly dressed and moccasins without sox."

"A surprising climate. We have not had one cold day since we passed the "great shute". The only change we experienced is from fair weather to rainy, windy weather."

The day before Christmas: "--the greater part of the men moved into their huts--Joe Fields finished for Captain Lewis and myself, each, a wide slab hued to write on. Joe Fields finished a table and seats for us."

"Huts smoke very bad."

One room at the Fort was assigned to Charbonneau, Sacajawea and their baby. There was just one double bed. Baby Jean Baptiste, "Pomp", would have slept with his parents.

Christmas Day was observed   "--we awoke by the discharge of the firearms of all our party and a salute, shouts and a song which the whole party joined in under our window--our dinner consisted of poor elk, so much spoiled that we eat it through necessity."

NEW YEARS 1806 was greeted with firing of arms and shouts. "This was the only mark of respect which we had it in our power to pay this celebrated day-- solacing our thirst with our only beverage, pure water."

"The stockade was finished and the indians were informed that the gates would be closed at sunset and opene at sunrise."

"The water gate may be used freely by the garrison for the purpose of passing and repassing at all times."

"Each guard will every morning, after being relieved (from duty) furnish two loads of wood for the commading officers' fire. No tools to be kept out over night."

"Green pine wood burns very well if it is split."

"The hunters inform us that the elk are plentiful near the mountains 9 or 10 miles distant."

It is interesting to read that the indians had a small dog which they used only in hunting elk. The indians didn't eat dog flesh. The dogs were "--usually small-- are partly colored, black, white, brown and brindle. The head is long and nose pointed, eyes small, ears erect and pointed like those of the wolf, hair short and smooth except on the tail where it is as long as that of the cur dog and straight."

The indians rarely were successful in hunting the elk which were so plentiful in that area. The Journals list the different means of hunting which the indians along the Columbia used. The gun, the bow and arrow, dead-

falls, pits, snares, spears or gigs. Their guns generally
were inferior, old ones repaired for indian trade. There
was an occasional good piece. The indians did not
understand the care required to keep a gun in good
working order. They kept their powder in small japaned
tin flasks which came with their ammunition when
they bought the gun from the traders. When the indian
ran out of ball or shot they substituted gravel or
pieces of potmetal and seemed unaware of the damage
they did to their guns. The quiver for the arrows, when
using the bow and arrow, was usually the skin of
a young bear or that of a wolf--open at the side in-
stead of the end as the quivers generally are. This
construction appeared to answer better for the canoe.

Again there was noted a new mode of dress. The
lower Columbia River indian wore no clothing at all,
not even moccasins. The climate was too wet to wear
leather which rots when exposed to constant wetness.
But the indians did have woven cedar mats to wrap
around them in excessive weather, also handsome
woven cedar hats. Shredded cedar skirts were worn
occasionally by the older men and women. Strips of
animal fur, even feathers still attatched to the skin,
were intermingled with the shredded cedar for
ornamentation as were different kinds of grasses.
(Again the book CEDAR by Hilary Stewart is recommended.)

In the Journals we read (the Chinookan women have)

"--large legs and thighs which are generally swelled from stoppage of the circulation in the feet (which are small) by many strands of beads--drawn tight around the ankles."

"The Chinookan women are lude and carry on sport publicly. The Clatsops and others appear diffident and reserved."

"These people (are) fond of cold, hot vapor baths of which they make frequent use both in sickness and in health and at all seasons of the year--they have a custom of bathing themselves all over with urine every morning."

"The Clatsops, Chinooks, Tillamooks all are very loquacious and inquisitive. They posses good memories. They are generally cheerful but never gay--notwithstanding the servile (manner) in which the (men) treat their women they pay much more respect to their judgement and opinion in many respects than most indian nations. Their women are permitted to speak freely before them and sometimes appear to command with a tone of authority."

"The natives are extravagantly fond of the most common, cheap blue beads of moderate size--the blue is usually preferred to the white. These beads constitute the principal circulating medium with all the indian tribes on this river. For these beads they will dispose (of) any article they posses. The beads are strung on strands of a fathom (6 feet) in length and in that manner sold by the breadth or yard."

"--the Clatsop indians appear much neater in their diet than indians are commonly, and frequently wash their faces and hands." Towels were made of soft, shredded cedar bark.

"The sun rose fair this morning for the first time for six weeks past. The clouds soon obscured it from view and a shower of rain succeeded."

"This day proved to be the fairest and best which we have had since our arrival at this place, only 3 showers during this whole day--."

"The coast in the neighborhood of Clark's Mountain (Tillamook Head) is slipping off and falling into the ocean in immense masses. Fifty or a hundred acres at a time give way and a great portion in an instant percipitated into the ocean--this splitting assunder at this time is no doubt caused by the incessant rains which have fallen within the last two months."

Before leaving this minutia something should be said about the flattening of the Chinookan infant's head. That practice became a conflict when Chinookan indian women married white men. The white man would not tolerate having his child's head deformed and in the eyes of a Chinookan, any human who did not have a flattened head was automatically classed a slave.

Narcissa Whitman noted in 1836 "I saw a child about a year old whose head had been recently released from its pressure--all the back part of it was a purple color as if it had been sadly bruised. We are told this custom is wearing away fast, there is only a few tribes on this river (Columbia) who practice it."

Practicing accuracy was also a part of this amazing Expedition. JAN. 31,1806. "The days of month are correct but the days of the week are wrong. This error we now correct."

But not all things could be corrected. An overnight snow fall on January 28th changed the landscape so completely the men could not find the animals they had killed the previous day.

The salt makers had set up a comfortable convenient camp and could produce 3 quarts to a gallon a day "--excellent, strong and white (salt)."

For seven weeks the salt makers, with 5 kettles, boiled down the sea water to extract the salt. But health problems plagued their camp. Bratton was very unwell and Gibson was so sick that he could not sit up or walk alone. Willard had cut his knee badly with a tomahawk.

"--sent Pryor with a party of 4 men in a canoe to bring Gibson to the fort. As Bratton had been sick we desire him to return to the fort also if he thought proper."

Gibson began to recover. Bratton developed an obstinate cough and pain in his back and appeared to be getting weaker. Willard, who cut his knee with a tomahawk "--has a high fever and complains of the pain in his head and want of appetite."

The men who were well enough to work were busy dressing elk skins for clothing but had difficulty because the brain of the elk wasn't sufficient to fully dress one hide and there wasn't soap to offset the deficiency and there weren't ashes enough to produce lye to make soap. To do authentic "indian tanning" only the brains are used and the brain of a deer is the exact amount needed to tan its hide, not so for elk.

Many times elk were shot so far away from the Fort and so late in the day that the meat could not be picked up until the following day. One time 5 elk had been left to be picked up. Two elk had been brought in. The following day the hunters discovered that the indians had stollen the remaining 3. "--I find that these people will all steal." Six days later a Clatsop man brought 3 dogs in payment for the elk which he and others had stolen. "However, the dogs took the alarm and ran off." The indians were given shelter at the Fort over night.

The large indian canoe was much admired by the men of the Expedition. Those canoes were upward of 50 feet long and could carry 8 to 10 thousand pounds of cargo. Twenty to thirty people could also be accommodated in its size. Those canoes were generally made of white cedar but sometimes fir. One of the men of the party purchased a much needed canoe from one of the indians. He had to give one of Captain Lewis' uniform, laced coats and nearly half a carrot of tobacco. "--a canoe is an article of the greatest value except a wife with whom it is equal--."

Captain Lewis complained in his Journals that he felt he should be reimbursed by the government of the United States for that coat as it had been little worn. He was reimbursed.

One morning the sergeant of the guard reported the absence of their indian canoe. On inquiry the captains learned that the men who came in with it last evening had been negligent in securing her and the tide-- had taken her off. "We sent a party down to the bay in search of her. They returned unsuccessful--this being a considerable loss she is so light that 4 men can carry her on their shoulders a mile or more without resting and will carry 3 men and from 12 to 15 hundred pound:

Later we learn the indian canoe "--so long lost and lamented was accidentally found."

"WE are infested with swarms of fleas already in our new habitation--we shall never divest ourselves of this troublesome vermin. Fleas are so abundant that we have to have them killed out of our blankets every day or get no sleep at night."

"The indians have different houses and villages to which they remove frequently to get rid of (the fleas) and not withstanding all their precautions they never step into our hut without leaving swarms of those troublesome insects. The first of those insects we saw on the Columbia River was at the first great falls, (Celilo Falls).

There were 3 principal roots which the indians used for food : wappato (even the indians paid a high price for it). A black root "is the root of the edible thistle, the first year's growth--that has one straight root something like a parsnip. It is tender, sweet and palatable, plus the wild liquorice."

Cranberries were bought, also mats "neatly made of flags and rushes--a hat made of splits and strong grass, also small baskets to hold water made of splits and straw--for those articles we gave high prices--we were unable to purchase (some things) without reducing our stock of merchandise on which we depend for our return trip."

"This evening we exhausted the last of our candles, but fortunately had taken the precaution to bring with us molds and wick. We do not yet consider ourselves destitute of this necessary article."

"A Clatsop man, his wife and a small boy, about 10 years old (a slave who, the man informed me was his cook, offered to sell him to me for beads and a gun. Those people brought some anchovies (smelt), sturgeon, beaver robe and some roots for sale. They asked such high prices for everything--we purchased part of a sturgeon for which we gave a few fishing hooks. We suffered them to stay the night."

The captains learned of a whale which had been washed up in the area of the Tillamook indians. The oil and blubber from that whale was highly esteemed by the indians.

Captain Clark set out with 2 canoes and 12 men to fir the whale in hopes of purchasing blubber. Charbonneau and Sacajawea were of that party and baby Pomp, too, who was still nursing. Only the skeleton remained, measuring 105 feet long. Reluctantly the indians sold 3 pounds of blubber and a few gallons of oil.

Poor health continued to be a worry. "Bratton is now weaker than any of the convalescents. He complains of a violent pain in the small of his back and is unable-- sit up. We give him one of our flannel shirts. I applied bandage of flannel to the part and rubbed it well with some volatile liniment which was prepared with spirits wine, camphor, castile soap, and a little laudanum. He felt better in the evening at which time I repeated th liniment and bathed his (feet) to restore circulation wh he complained of in that part."

Set Shields at work to make some sacks of elk skin tc

INK RENDERING BY SHIRLEY J. NIEMINEN PORTLAND, OREGON

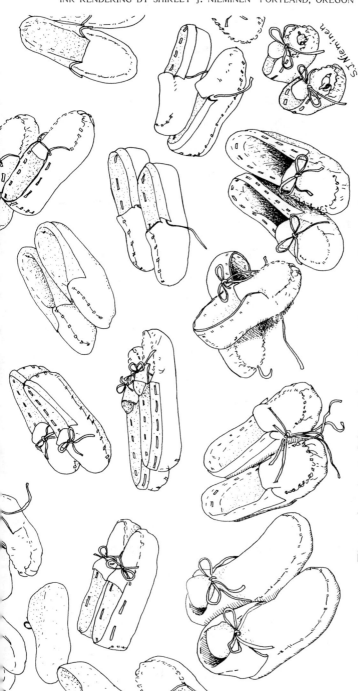

Three hundred fifty-eight pairs of maccasins made at Fort Clatsop for return journey. The preliminary sketches of the moccasins displeased the illustrator. "They don't walk," was her complaint. She overcame that. Note infant moccasins at lower right-hand corner.

contain various articles.

"Our party are now furnished with 358 pairs of moccasins--a good portion of dressed leather--also shirts, overalls, capotes of dressed elk-skin for the homeward journey."

"Drewyer was taken last night with a violent pain in his side. Captain Clark bled him. Several of the men are complaining of being unwell. It is truly unfortunate that they be sick at the moment of our departure."

The men of the party were thoughtful of each other. One returned after an unsuccessful day of hunting but brought cranberries for the sick.

All effort now was made for the day of departure. The weather was so rainy and windy the men could not load the canoes but other tasks needed to be taken care of.

"This morning we gave Delashelwith (a Chinookan Chief) a certificate of his own good deportment and furnished him with a list of our names, after which we sent him home with all his female band. We have given such lists to several of the natives and posted a copy in our own quarters. Our object in so doing we stated in the preamble of this muster-roll as follows:

> "The object of this list is, that through
> the medium of some civilized person
> whose names are hereunto annexed, and
> who were sent out by the government of
> the United States in May 1804, to explore

the interior of the Continent of North America, did penetrate the same by way of the Missouri and Columbia Rivers, to the discharge of the latter into the Pacific Ocean, where they arrived on the 14th of November 1805, and from whence they departed the (23rd day of March 1806) on their return to the United States by the same route they had come out."

One copy of that document did find its way out of Fort Clatsop. On page 903, Vol III, Couse we read, (it)   "--fell into the possession of Captain Hill, who while on the coast of the Pacific, procured it from the natives. This note accompanied him on his voyage to Canton whence it arrived in the United States."

"Ross Cox, an Astorian by sea in the "Beaver" who reached the Columbia in April 1812 visited Fort Clatsop. The logs of the houses were still standing, and marked with the names of several of the party."

In 1834 J.K. Townsend, a noted naturalist observed, "October 14th, I walked today around the beach to the foot of Young's Bay--to see the remains of the house in which Lewis and Clark's party resided--the logs of which it was composed are still perfect, but the roof of bark has disappeared and the whole vicinity is over grown with thorn and wild currant bushes--."

This same Townsend wrote of the Chinooks "Whatever may be said derogatory of these people I can testify that inhospitality is not among the numbers of their failings."   But the Chinook dog.   "fierce brutes who are not half as hospitable as their masters," was the reaction of Dr. R.B. Hinds in 1838 assistant surgeon on the British ship, "Sulphur."

In the early 1840s or early 50s there was a small saw-mill on the site. Remember what Patrick Gass wrote, "--the straightest most beautifulest logs--."

Francis Fuller Victor in her book "All Over Oregon and Washington" published in 1872 wrote "--the site being overgrown with trees 20 feet in height--nothing now remains except immense beds of half-rotted saw-dust, embedding one or two charred foundation timbers."

To return to the Corps of Discovery. Many indians came to say good-bye. To Commowool, Chief of the Clatsops (who) "had been the most kind and hospitable of all the indians in this quarter, we therefore gave him a certif-icate of the kindness and attention which we had re-ceived from him, and added a more substatial proof of our gratitude, the gift of all our houses and furniture."

"The rains and winds still confined us to our fort, but at last our provisions dwindled down to a single day's stock and it became absolutely necessary to remove. We therefore sent a few hunters ahead and stopped (caulked) the boats as well as we could with mud."

MARCH 23, 1806: "This morning proved so rainy and uncertain that we were undetermined for sometime whether we had best set out--the rain ceased and it became fair about meridian, at which time we loaded our canoes and at 1 p.m. left Fort Clatsop on our homeward bound journey. At this place we had wintered and remained from the 7th of December, 1805 to this day and have lived as well as we had any right to expect and we can say that we were never one day without 3 meals of some kind a day, either poor elk meat or roots." From December 1,1805 to March 20,1806 the men had killed 131 elk and 20 deer.

In an interesting footnote we read, "They (the captains) are still remembered by the older indians. One of these indians told a settler that the captains were real chiefs and that the Americans who had come since were common people."

That concept has quietly lingered all these long years. In June 1989 this person had the privilege of attending an unveiling, in traditional indian ceremony, of 4 new totem poles. One of those poles was the LEWIS AND CLARK totem pole representing two chiefs in honored position at the top of the pole, a stylized handsome rendering of the traditional cedar hats of royalty.

Those poles belong to the Cascade Geographic Society of Rhododendron, Oregon.

Hunting continued to be a daily chore and meat not needed for immediate consumption was dried for future use. The dried meat of 4 elk was brought into camp but it had not been sufficiently dried and that evening it had to be cut thinner and redried over the fire.

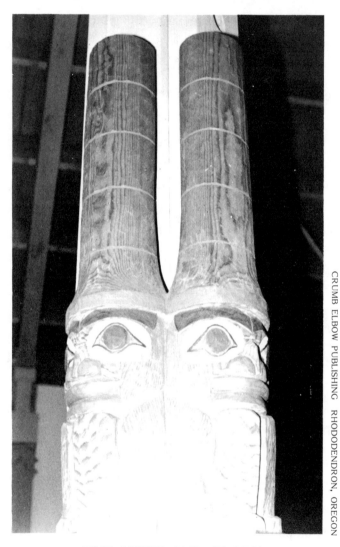

CRUMB ELBOW PUBLISHING   RHODODENDRON, OREGON

THE LEWIS AND CLARK
TOTEM POLE

Two chiefs in honored position at the top of
the pole, a stylized handsome rendering of
the traditional cedar hats of royalty.

"They (the captains) are still remembered by the older indians. One of these indians told a settler that the captains were real chiefs and that the Americans who had come since were common people."
  (pole belongs to the Cascade Geographic Society of Rhododendron, Oregon)

"We had the meat cut into thin pieces and scaffold with a fire under it to dry it, which we expect in the course of the night can be effected." Deerskins which had been prepared to store the dried meat also needed additional drying, a detail which was promptly taken care of.

Three bear cubs were brought into camp abandoned by their mother. The indians very much wanted them and a good exchange was made for wappato.

The Expedition again passed the Quicksand (Sandy) River. The fir tree pictured was 140 years old when Lewis and Clark were at Quicksand River on their Homeward Journey. That fir tree, as the crow flys, was only about 10 miles away. The tree was felled in 1946 on property adjoining ours: 6 1/2 foot on the stump, 225 feet long, 60 feet to the first limb, 237 years old. (picture, by Clara Sisson, now deceased)

One day when the Corps was traveling the south side of the Columbia River it discovered that there had been a recent fire which had caused the fir trees to

release quantities of pitch which the men collected
to use on their boats. Remember, when leaving Fort
Clatsop the only caulking available was mud.

The fatigues, the physical exhaustion, the aggravation
brought on by indian behavior plagued the Expedition as
it battled the current up river. Two indians met with
John Shields "--and pushed him out of the road. He
had nothing to defend himself with except a large knife
which he drew with an intention of putting one or
both of them to death before they could get themselves in readiness to use their arrows. They fled
through the woods."

Three indians stole Captain Lewis' dog but fled when
they saw three men of the Corps following them. An
ax was stollen but wrested away. The indians were
informed, "--if any further attempts to steal our
property or insult our men we should put them to
instant death." "I am convinced that no other con-
sideration but our number at this moment protects us."

"We caused all the men of the party who had short
guns to carry them on the portage for fear of some
attempt on the part of the natives to rob the party."
"--our men seem well disposed to kill a few of them."

All the while Sacajawea and her baby were part of this
turmoil. Very little is written about Sacajawea in the
Journals. If only she, too, could have kept a Journal.

The indian traffic was heavy on the river as the indians were setting up camps in preparation for the spring salmon run. To make camp was not simple for those people. It meant taking down the boards of their permanent houses, including the bark used for the roofs, loading it all into their canoes along with their families, household effects, storage baskets, fishing gear, and whatever else they needed.

Those temporary houses were not sunk into the ground but merely served as shelters for the duration of the salmon run.

The Corps made slow progress against that swift flowing river. Only 7 miles in three days on an especially difficult stretch. Dogs were purchased for food whenever available as the men found that their physical strength was greater on a diet of dog meat than lean elk or deer or horse meat. Might that be that the diet of a dog is also flesh rather than vegetation?

After portaging the "long shute" and getting into less wooded country, horses became evident and the serious business of bartering for horses became a daily task. The indians asked nearly half the merchandise that the captains had for one horse. Food and wood had to be bought from the indians which dwindled the Corps' supply of trade goods which was minimal to begin with.

Elk skins were put in water to make harnesses for the

packhorses but not cut until the number of horses were known.

In time 8 horses were purchased and packsaddles made up for 7 horses, the 8th, Bratton was compelled to ride as he was yet unable to walk. Two canoes proceeded up the Columbia "--with all the baggage which could not be carried on horseback."

The Dalles was a most unhappy segment of the return journey. Patrick Gass wrote, "I think the present is the only occasion on which either of the captains was forced to assault and battery."

The Dalles was a conglomerate of good and evil. It was the hub of commerce for indians coming along trails from many directions , plus the river traffic coming from up river and down. Many ugly incidents and frustrations are recorded in the Journals during this regrettable layover on the journey home. There is an interesting footnote in Vol III of Couse, page 959 which compares the Columbia River indians with the Sioux on the Missouri classifying the two of them as "river pirates."

With the unpleasantness at The Dalles behind them the Corps of Discovery looked forward to a restful stopover with the Walla Walla indians and their distinguished Chief Yellept. On the way down the Columbia the captains couldn't accept the invitation to stayover because the Corps had to find a suitable camp before winter set in. But the captains promised Chief Yellept that they would stop on the return journey which they did. "--these friendly, honest people" even three days after leaving the Walla Wallas, three young men of that villaage arrived "--bringing with them a steel trap belonging to one of our party which had been negligently left behind. This is an act of integrity rarely witnessed among indians. During our stay with them they several times found the knives of the men which had been carelessly lost by them and returned them. I think we can justly affirm to the honor of these people that they are the most hospitable, honest, and sincere people that we have met with in our voyage."

The captains took time to record an interesting indian custom, "I observe a small lodge with one fire, which seems to be the retreat of their women in a certain situation (menses). The men are not permitted to approach this lodge within a certain distance, and if they have anything to convey to the occupants of this little hospital they stand at the distance of 50 or 60 paces and throw it towards them as far as they can and retire.

"This man has a daughter now arrived at the age of puberty who being (in) a certain situation, is not per-mitted to associate with the family but sleeps at dis-tance from her father's camp and when traveling follows at some distance behind. In this state I am informed that the female is not permitted to eat, nor touch any article of a culinary nature--."

Mosquitoes became the great tormentors again. "--was so troublesome to the men last night that they slept very little. My mosquito beir has a number of small holes worn through (which) they pass in. --the mosquitoes so numerous that I could not keep them off my gun long enough to take sight and by that means missed--a light breeze of wind which continued all the forepart of the night from the southwest and blew away the mosquitoes.

"The child of Charbonneau has been much bitten by the mosquitoes that his face is much puffed up and swelled."

Long years after Lewis and Clark, to avoid similar mosquito misery on my pre-school son berry picking on mosquito infested Sauvies Island (Wappato Island of Lewis and Clark and indian era) a remedy had been suggested. Liquid bluing would instantly aleviate all stinging and itching and swelling. Being a thoughtful mother a bottle of that bluing was brought along in the picnic basket. Whenever my son came to me with a mosquito bite the bottle of bluing would be agitated to moisten the cork. A beautiful round circle of blue was immediately applied to the mosquito bite. It worked!! No itching. No stinging. No swelling. By the end of the day he was a strange looking little boy with blue circles all over his face and neck and hands. A friend, being told of this wonderful remedy became instantly alarmed. Something in the blue dye could have been harmful. Maybe luck didn't end with the Corps of Discovery.

"--a wolf bit Sergeant Pryor through his hand when asleep--Shannon shot (the wolf). Sergeant Pryor's hand has nearly recovered."

There was an interesting statement in the Journals dated August 22, 1806. A Cheyenne Chief "--requested me (Clark) to send some traders to them, that their country was full of beaver and they would then be encouraged to kill beaver, but now they had no use for them as they could get nothing for their skins and did not know well how to catch beaver. If the white people would come amongest them they would become acquainted and they (the white people) would learn them how to take the beaver."

Mention should be made of the bullboats, a marvelous Mandan method of transportation. They were made of sticks and green buffalo hide. Sergeant Pryor had cause to make and use 2 of them in an emergency. The instructions for making were carefully noted and included in the Journals.

Food continued to be a problem as the Corps made its way to Nez Perce country. Along the way stories were heard of famine the previous winter. Some tribes were forced to boil and eat moss growing on the pine trees. In one area many pine trees were down. The indians had to drop them to get to the cones which housed the seeds which were roasted or boiled for food. In size those seeds are similar to sunflower seeds.

THE FAMOUS MANDAN BULLBOAT

"--2 sticks of 1 1/4 inch diameter is tied together so as to form a round hoop of the size
you wish the canoe, or as large as the skin
will allow to cover. Two of those hoops are
made, one for the top or brim and the other
for   the bottom to the depth you wish the
canoe. Then sticks of the same size are crossed at right angles and fastened with a thong
to each hoop and also where each stick crosses
each other. Then the skin, when green, is drawn
tight over this frame and fastened with thongs
to the brim or outer hoop so as to form a
perfect basin. One of those canoes will carry
6 or 8 men and their loads."

This person remembers similar stories handed down in her family of a famine in Sweden where people went to the forests to get bark to eat.

"A man produced 2 canisters of powder which he informed us he had found by means of his dog where they had been buried--near the river. They were the same which we had buried as we descended the river last fall As he kept them safe and had honesty enough to return them to us we gave him a fire steel by way of compensation. A footnote taken from Patrick Gass' journal reads, "All the indians from the Rocky Mountains to the Falls of the Columbia are an honest, ingenious and well-disposed people, but from the falls to the sea coast, and along it, they are a rascally, thieving set."

Food continued to be scarce for the indians as well as the Corps of Discovery. But whenever the hunters brought in meat, the captains shared with the indians. Two deer were brought in, each with unborn twins which were given to the indians who boiled them whole including hide, hair and entrails and in that condition ate them.

On reaching the Nez Perce the chiefs recommended a site across the Clearwater River which at one time had been an indian camp but had been abandoned for some time. "---nothing remained but a circle 30 yards in diameter sunk in the ground about 4 feet with a wall around it--nearly 3 1/2 feet in height. In this place we deposited our baggage and around its edges formed our tents of sticks and grass."

"--the party formed themselves very comfortable tents with willow poles and grass in the form of the awning of a wagon. These were made perfectly secure as well from the heat of the sun as from rain. We had a bower constructed for ourselves under which we sit by day and sleep under the part of an old sail--." A footnote states that the Nez Perce made wickiups of brush and grass which were impervious to rain.

As the Corps settled down for the 5 weeks wait for the snow to melt in the mountains a routine set in. "Great numbers of indians apply to us for medical aid which we gave them cheerfully so far as our skill and store of medicine would enable us. Scrofula, ulcers , rheumatism , sore eyes, and the loss of the use of their limbs are the most common cases among them." Captain Clark soon had a line of 50 indians waiting.

"Sacajawea gathered quantity of the roots of a species of fennel which we found very agreeable food, the flavor of this root is not unlike anise seed and they dispel the wind which the roots called cows and quamash (camas) are apt to create particularly the latter. We also boil a small onion (with our meat) which we find in great abundance--the mush of the roots we find adds much comfort to our diets."

"Our indian woman was busily engaged today in laying in a store of the fennel roots for the Rocky Mountains."

"My object is to procure as many skins as possible for

the purpose of purchasing corn and beans of the Mandan; as we have now no articles of merchandise nor horses to purchase with, our only resort is skins which those people were very fond of the winter we were stationed near them."

As the Corps made its way eastward to reach the Nez Perce the party met many greatful indians whom the captains had doctored on their outward journey. The captains were pleased with these warm memories, "--highly servicable in preparing the minds of the natives for our reception." After the hostilities along the Columbia the captains needed reassurance.

Captain Clark noticed an indian with a broken arm wrapped loosely in a piece of leather with no support to assist healing. The arm was set, splinted and cradled in a sling.

Ulcers and skin erruptions were tended to and always there was need for "eye-water." Eye problems were an accepted misery among the indians resulting many times in early blindness. Perhaps the indians' restricted diet had something to do with it in adddition to venereal diseases.

Something should be said here about communication and translation which was a tedious, uncertain process. The procedure started in English to one of the Corps who could speak French to Charbonneau who interpreted to Sacajawea who spoke in Shoshoni to a Shoshoni prisoner who translated into Nez Perce. A long path and we think much is lost in one translation.

Doctoring became vital to the Corps' subsistance as there was scarcely any merchandise left for barter. Healing the sick could be used in exchange for food and supplies. Roots were part of this exchange. "Cow-as" "Cous" "Cows" "Cow-weed" was a root reasonably agreeable to the men's stomachs. The Journals give a detailed description of "cows."

> "This cows is a knobbed root of an irreg-
> ular form, rounded not unlike gensing.
> This root they collect, rub off a thin,
> black rind which covers it and pounding
> it, expose it to the sun. Those cakes are
> about 1 1/4 inches thick and 6 to 18 in-
> ches in width. When dried they either
> eat this bread alone without any further
> preparation or boil it and make a thick
> mucelage. This latter is most common
> and much the most agreeable."

The Journals mention that the men of the Corps could have collected the roots of cows but there were several species of (water) hemlock growing among the cows and the men dared not risk it. Hemlock is deadly poisonous.

Baby Pomp was teething and became dangerously ill with "--jaw and back of neck swollen and a high tem-perature." Hot onion poultices were applied, plus "--a plaster of salve made of the rosin of the long-leafed pine, beeswax and bear's oil." In time Baby Pomp re-covered.

But the greatest healing which lingered the longest in the memory of the indians was the miraculous recovery of one of their chiefs.

It all began with Bratton who became ill at the salt-makers' camp along the Pacific Ocean in present Seaside., Oregon back in mid February 1806. Here he was, four months later, at the foothills of the Bitterroot Mountains still unable to walk, work, or even have one free hour of pain in his lower back.

The Journals continue:

> "W. Bratton is yet very low. He eats heartily but he is so weak in the small of his back that he can't walk. We have made use of every remedy to restore him without its having the desired effect. One of our party, John Shields, observed that he had seen men in similar symptons restored by violent sweats and Bratton requested that he be sweated in the way Shields proposed, which we agreed to. Shields dug a round hole 4 feet deep and 3 feet in diameter in which he made a large fire so as to heat the hole after which the fire was taken out a seat was placed in the hole, the patient was then set on the seat with a board under his feet and a can of water handed him to throw on the bottom and sides of the hole so as to create as great a heat as he could bear and the hole covered with blankets supported by hoops. After about 20 minutes the patient was taken out and put in cold water a few minutes and returned to the hole in which he was kept about 1 hour, then taken out and covered with several blankets, which was taken off by degrees until he became cool. This remedy took place yesterday and Bratton is walking about today and is much better than he has been.
>
> "At 11 a.m. a canoe came down with the indian

man who had applied for medical assistance while we lay at the Broken Arms village. This man I had given a few doses of flower of sulphur and creme of tartar and directed that he should take the cold bath every morning. He had lost the use of all his limbs and his fingers are contracted. We are at a loss to determine what to do for this unfortunate man. I gave him a few drops of ladanum and some portsble soup as medicine.

(The next day) "We caused a sweat to be prepared for the indian chief in the same manner in which Bratton had been sweated. This we attempted but were unable to succeed as he was unable to sit up or be supported in the place. We informed the indians that we knew of no relief for him except sweating him in their sweat houses and giving him plenty of the tea of the horse mint which we showed them and they probably would not succeed as he had been so long in his present situation. I am confident that this would be an excellent subject for electricity and much regret that I have it not in my power to supply it.

(The next day) "The indians were so anxious that the sick chief should be sweated under our inspection that they requested we would make a second attempt today. Accordingly the hole was somewhat enlarged and his father a very good-looking old man went into the hole with him and sustained him in a proper position during the operation. We could not make him sweat as copiously as we wished. After the operation he complained of considerable pain. We gave him 30 drops of ladanum which soon composed him and he rested very well.

"This is at least a strong mark of paternal affection. They all appear extremely attentive to this sick man. He has been sick and helpless upwards of 3 years. The Nez Perce appear to be very attentive and kind to their aged people and treat their women with more respect than the nations of the Missouri.

(The following day) "The sick chief was much better this morning. He can use his hands and arms and seems much pleased with the prospect of recovering. He says he feels much better than he has for a great number of months. We have consented that he should still remain with us and repeat these sweats. He sits up a great proportion of the day."

"The chief has much more use of his hands and arms. He washed his face himself today which he has been unable to do previously for more than 12 months. Bratton is recovering his strength very fast."

"We gave the sick chief a severe sweat today. Shortly after which he could move one of his legs and thighs and work his toes pretty well. The other leg he can move a little. His fingers and arms seem to be almost entirely restored. He seems highly delighted with his recovery."

"The indian chief appears to be gradually recovering the use of his limbs."

"We gave the indian chief another sweat today, continuing it as long as he could possibly bear it. In the evening he was very languid but appeared still to improve in the use of his limbs."

"The sick chief is fast on the recovery. He can bear his weight on his legs. Bratton has so far recovered that we cannot consider him an invalid any longer. He has had a tedious illness which he bore with much fortitude and firmness."

To have witnessed the curing of those two invalids would have been a marvalous experience. There is a picture of that chief's daughter, 110 years old, taken in 1901, who remembers Lewis and Clark among the Nez Perce in 1806 and the astonishing cure of her father. This picture is on page 116 in

"To The Pacific With Lewis And Clark" by Ralph K. Andrist.

The Journals continue: "The day came when we could attempt the crossing of the Rockies. Without the skill and intelligence of our indian guides we would have perished.

"An interesting superstition was practiced our first night out. Fir trees were set on fire. The trees have a great number of dry limbs along the lower part of their trunks which when set on fire create a very sudden and immense blaze from the bottom to the top. The affect was like fireworks. The reason was to bring fair weather for our journey.

"The traveling was hazardous over snow 7 to 10 feet deep. The horses would slip and slide but their feet never sunk deeper than 2 or 3 inches into the snow. As treacherous as this was we made better time and the traveling was easier than picking our way over fallen timber and rocks.

"We were much pleased to recognize camp sites where we had stopped on our way west. For 7 exhausting days we battled those immense mountains. One time our pack horses had no food or their packs removed from their backs for 28 tortuous miles. How greatful we were when we could finally bid the snow adieu and rest our horses and ourselves.

The time came for our guides to leave us and they showed every emotion of regret. They insisted in exchanging names with Captain Lewis according to their custom. Captain Lewis was given the indian name YOMEKOLIK which means "The White Bear Skin Folded" in honor of the grizzly. The hunters were set out to get meat for our guides who had conducted us through those tremendous mountains.

"Eight days later we were in buffalo country and they were mating which keeps the bulls in a tremendous roar. We can hear them for miles. Our horses have not known buffalo and are alarmed at their appearance and the bellowing. In one area there were at least 10,000 within a circle of 2 miles.

We encountered a party of 8 indians with horses who appeared cautious but friendly. We did not trust them even though we camped that night together. In the morning I was awakened by Drewyer shouting, "Dam you, let go my gun." I saw Reuben and Joseph Fields overtake an indian running with their guns. In the scuffle, Reuben Fields stabbed the indian in the heart. In the meantime an indian seized my and Drewyer's guns and began driving off the horses. I shouted for them to give back my horse or I would shoot. Drawing my pistol I shot the indian through the belly. The indian dropped to his knees and from that position fired. I felt the wind of the bullet as it passed over my head.

The indians fled, leaving half their horses and most of their weapons. While I burned the indians bows and arrows and shields on the campfire the other men saddled up and we rode off fast as our horses could go.

Fearing reprisal we rode until 2 o'clock that night with the aid of a bright moon, taking only 2 short rests.

"One day we saw a herd of elk in some willows. Cruzatte and I went ashore. We both shot one. We reloaded our guns and went in different directions. I was in the act of firing when a bullet passed through my left thigh. It was very severe but it had missed the bone. I called out, "Dam you, you shot me." I had to conclude that Cruzatte had mistaken me for an elk as I was dressed in brown leather and Cruzatte was blind in one eye and nearsighted in the other. I called several times (but) received no answer. Cruzatte was only 40 paces away and could have heard but when he didn't answer I concluded that an indian had shot me.

"In great pain I ran toward the canoe calling as loud as I could for Cruzatte to do the same as there were indians around. When I was in sight of the pirogue I called the men to get their guns as I was wounded by an indian and to follow me to rescue Cruzatte from the indians.

"The men followed with their guns. Within a hundred paces my wounds became so painful and my thigh so stiff I could continue no further. I ordered the men to proceed but if they found themselves overpowered or outnumbered to retreat but keep up their fire.

"I got back to the pirogue as well as I could and got my pistol, rife and air gun in order determined to sell my life as dearly as possible. In this state of anxiety and suspense I waited.

"Twenty minutes later the men returned with Cruzatte. They had seen no indians nor any trace of any. Cruzatte seemed much alarmed and swore he had not shot me, that he had shot an elk. I asked if he hadn't heard when I called. He absolutely denied that he had. I do not believe that he did it intentionally, but the bullet lodged in my breeches was of the short rifles that he ha

"With assistance of Sergeant Gass I took off my clothes and dressed my wounds myself as well as I could, inserting patent lint into the ball holes. The wounds bled considerably but I was greatful it had touched neither bone nor artery. It was painful for me to be removed from the pirogue, therefore I stayed on board. The wounds excited a high fever and I had a very uncomfortable night.

"My wounds felt stiff and sore but there was much less inflamation than I expected. That evening I supplied a poultice of Peruvian barks.

"As writing in my present situation is extremely painful to me I shall have Captain Clark continue the Journal."

"I treated the wounds of my friend and 2 days later were back with the Mandan indians where we spent our first winter. Now the time had come to say goodbye to Charbonneau, Sacajawea and Pompy. Charbonneau was officially discharged and paid $500.33 (and) 1/3 cents. Sacajawea received nothing but I offered to

take Pompy to St. Louis and educate him. Charbonneau felt the child was too young to leave his mother,
but in a year they would bring him to me."

They did bring Baptiste to Clark and in Clark's personal
records as late as 1820 he was paying for Baptiste's
education. Three years later a young twenty-year-old
Prince from Germany met Baptiste, liked him and took
him to Europe with him. The two of them didn't return
to America until six years later. Baptiste by then was a
well educated, polished gentleman who could converse
fluently in 4 languages. But Baptiste could not stay
away from the wilderness he had been born to and became a guide as his father had been, even serving as a
guide for Captain Clark's son and a nephew. At the age
of 60 Baptiste Charbonneau died of mountain fever and
is buried near Danner, Oregon. His death was recorded
in 3 separate newspapers, one in Idaho, two in Califor-
nia. (page 174 "Sacajawea" by Harold P. Howard.)

But to get back to the Journals.
Captain Clark writes: "Captain Lewis recovers slowly.
Ahead of us lay the Teton Sioux. One day we met a
party of them, even their chief, Black Buffalo, who
attempted to detain us coming up the Missouri. I told
them that they were bad people, that they had treated
us poorly two years ago, and that they had abused all
the whites who had visited them since, and they were
to return to their camp and if any of them came near
our camp we would kill them. They went on their way.

Seven of them stopped on the top of the hill telling us to come across and they would kill us. One gave three strokes on the earth with his gun, a great oath among indians.

"When we reached Floyd's bluff we ascended the hill to pay respects to our buried campanion. We found that the grave had been opened by the indians and left half covered. We filled it and returned to our canoes.

"Captain Lewis has recovered from his wounds. He can walk and even run as well as ever he could.

"We meet many different parties on their way up the Missouri to trade with the indians. Their licenses are in good order except for one young man.

"One day we saw cows on the river bank which caused a shout of joy from our men.

"On September 23, 1806 we reached St. Louis, two year four months and 8,000 miles after we had departed. The entire town turned out to welcome us. We fired our gun in salute."

FOR THOSE WHO
HELPED
ALONG THE WAY

Deep appreciation to E.G. "Frenchy" Chuinard, M.D.
of Lacey, Washington for his calm guidance in moments
of hysteria. To the Oregon City Library for generous use
of the "Journals of Lewis and Clark" by Reuben Gold
Thwaites. To the Damascus Branch of the Clackamas
County Library for its careful monitoring of renewal
dates to keep this project on track. To friends who
mailed clippings pertinent to Lewis and Clark. To the
Washington State Historical Society for the picture
"Crossing the Bitter Root Mountains 1855" by Gustav
Sohon. Although that picture was painted half a
century after Lewis and Clark, the ruggedness of
the mountains remained the same. A special thanks
to the Washington State Parks and Recreation Commission, Olympia, Washington for permission to re-
produce the map from the booklet "Lewis and Clark
in the Fort Columbia Area." To my family for books
"which might be helpful." To Vern Erickson (from
"On A Slant Indian Village") for the drawing of
indian women on a corn-watching scaffold, Fort
Abraham Lincoln State Park, North Dakota. McLean
County Historical Society, Washburn, North Dakota
for permission to do an ink rendering of their
reconstructed Fort Mandan. To the National Park
Service, Ft. Clatsop National Memorial, Astoria,
Oregon for the picture of reconstructed Fort
Clatsop. To Lois Kemp, Mt. Hood National Forest,
Gresham, Oregon for information on the wappato
root. To Shirley Neiminen of Portland, Oregon
for the exquisite ink drawings which grace
this book. To Robert K. Brown of New Mexico
for his ink rendering of Crossing the Rockies.

B I B L I O G R A P H Y

This bibliography is limited to works frequently referred to. For greater in-depth
study, E.G. "Frenchy" Chuinard, M.D. has
granted permission to recommend the
scholarly bibliography in his book
ONLY ONE MAN DIED. As a person
reads the publication dates of some of
those references one becomes aware of
a patient silence, a waiting for hands to
turn fragile pages permitting the past
to once again become the present.

Andrist, R.K. TO THE PACIFIC WITH LEWIS AND
CLARK, American Heritage Publishing Co. Inc. 1967.
Bakeless, John THE JOURNALS OF LEWIS AND CLARK
    Mentor Books, 1964.
Chuinard, E.G. "Frenchy", M.D. ONLY ONE MAN DIED,
    Arthur H. Clark Co. 1979.
Coues, Elliott, HISTORY OF THE EXPEDITION UNDER
THE COMMAND OF LEWIS AND CLARK, Francis
    P. Harper, NY 1893.
DeVoto, Bernard THE JOURNALS OF LEWIS AND
CLARK, Houghton Mifflin Co. Boston, 1952.
Dillon R. MERIWETHER LEWIS, Coward McCann,Inc.
    1965.
Rees, John E. MADAME CHARBONNEAU, Lemhi
    County Historical Society, 1970. (vital reading to
    preserve the ethnic pronunciation of Sacajawea
    according to recorded history) 27 pages.
Snyder, Gerald S. IN THE FOOTSTEPS OF LEWIS AND
CLARK, Nat'l. Geog. Society, 1970.
Thwaites, R.G. ORIGINAL JOURNALS OF THE LEWIS
AND CLARK EXPEDITION, 8 vols, Dodd, Mead and
    Co. NY 1904-5.
WE PROCEEDED ON, 1974, all copies. The Quarterly
    Magazine of the Lewis and Clark Trail Heritage
    Foundation, Inc.